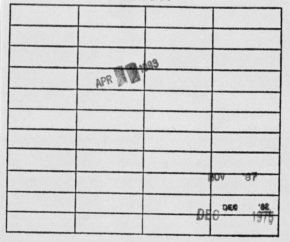

FLAMEWORKING

FLAMEWORKING

GLASSMAKING FOR THE CRAFTSMAN

FREDERIC SCHULER

CHILTON BOOK COMPANY

PHILADELPHIA · NEW YORK · LONDON

PUBLISHED IN PHILADELPHIA BY CHILTON BOOK COMPANY
and simultaneously in Ontario, Canada, by Thomas Nelson & Sons Ltd.

LIBRARY OF CONGRESS CATALOG CARD NUMBER 68-30863

DESIGNED BY HARRY EABY

MANUFACTURED IN THE UNITED STATES OF AMERICA

To Theophilus Rugerus, of the 12th century, who expressed my hopes and intentions most clearly in the preface to his book *The Various Arts*. "*Theophilus . . . wishes to all, who are willing to avoid and spurn idleness and the shiftlessness of the mind by the useful occupation of their hands and the agreeable contemplation of new things, the recompense of a heavenly reward!*"*

*Theophilus Rugerus. *The Various Arts*. Translated by C. R. Dodwell. London: Thomas Nelson and Sons, Ltd., 1961.

Author's Note

As Administrator of Scientific Research for the Corning Museum of Glass between 1956 and 1958, I have had the unique opportunity of observing glass blowers at work, talking and working with Frederick Carder, founder of Steuben Glass; having glass blowing lessons with Bill Johnson, Supervisor of B Factory, and studying and working on the duplication of ancient techniques. With Mr. Stanley Weisenfeld, Supervisor of Photo Media of the Corning Glass Works, I had a chance to photographically record details of the free-blowing process. The contact with the museum and its manifold artistic activities strengthened my interest in the arts and crafts.

I wish to thank Mr. Thomas Buechner, now Director of the Brooklyn Museum of Fine Arts, for his advice and criticism of my earliest attempts at writing on ancient techniques. The results of these efforts have appeared as articles in *Archeology*. I am grateful to Mr. Paul Perrot, Director of the Corning Museum of Glass, for his help with photographs, and Mr. Stanley Weisenfeld, Corning Glass Works, not only for his help with photographs for this book, but also for his help with our photo project on techniques. Great appreciation is extended to Mr. Jack Boydston, of Santa Barbara, for his help in photographing flameworking techniques and the finished pieces. Only a small fraction of this effort, unfortunately, appears in this book. Finally, I wish to thank Mr. Stanislaus Szukalski, my sculpturing teacher between 1960 and 1965, for his encouragement and advice.

Frederic Schuler
Santa Barbara

Contents

"But to shorten this comparison, I shall here set down the properties of glass, whereby any one may easily difference it from all other bodies.

'Tis a concrete of salt and sand or stones.

'Tis Artificial.

It melts in a strong fire.

When melted 'tis tenacious and sticks together.

'Tis ductile whilst red hot, and fashionable into any form, but not malleable, and may be blown into a hollowness.

'Tis friable when cold, which made our proverb, As brittle as glass.

It onely receives sculpture, and cutting, from a *Diamond* or *Emery* stone."*

*Antonio Neri. *The Art of Glass*, 1612,
translated by Christopher Merret in 1662

Part One

INTRODUCTION

1. The Uniqueness of Glass

Glass is a fascinating material. Objects of glass have a special aliveness in their transparency, colors, smooth surfaces, dynamic and changing effects when viewed under various lighting conditions and from different positions. The shaping techniques which involve fluid glass are equally exciting. There are two, flameworking and

Figure 1. "Pine Cone."

Figure 2. "Frog." Designed and carved by Erwin Burger. (*Glass 1959*)

free-blowing, each with a directness and intimacy in the working and shaping of glass. One marvels at holding a glass rod or tubing, then heating and forming the fluid center into a sparkling jewel (see figure 1). The remarkable physical properties of glass at high temperature impose almost no limits on its forms, which in the process of cooling become permanent.

Figure 3. Vase designed and engraved by John Hutton. (*Glass 1959*)

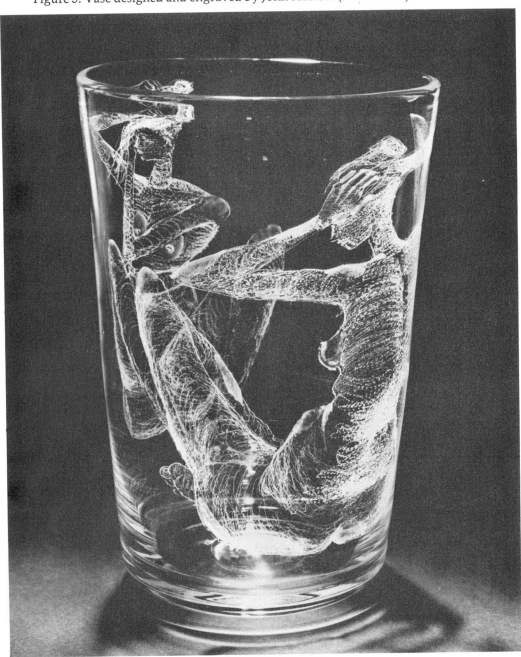

Cold glass can be shaped by grinding and polishing, using lapidary techniques. Thus the artist can alter or form pieces such as the imaginative "Frog" carved by Erwin Burger (see figure 2). One can roughen the surface, do diamond-point decoration, or copper-wheel engraving. For the latter, the design can be executed in line technique (see figures 3 and 4) or modeled in intaglio or relief. Some of these

Figure 4. Vase by John Hutton. *(Glass 1959)*

Figure 5. "Elk." Designed by Tapio Wirkkala, Corning Museum of Glass.

techniques can be combined. The piece can be carved and then decorated by copper-wheel engraving, as is the "Elk" designed by Tapio Wirkkala (see figure 5). Out of the special properties of glass come unique techniques.

6

2. Techniques for the Individual

This book will concentrate on flameworking techniques, but will describe both flameworking and free-blowing. The technique of flameworking, or reheating glass rod or tubing or other pieces of glass, was once called "lampworking." This method was used at least as early as 1660 to shape microscope lenses; the simple burners were derived from small oil lamps. With this technique, the glass was heated in a relatively small area where pieces were to be sealed, enlarged, or changed in some manner. The cool ends of the glass were held in the hands, which controlled the rotation and position of the fluid central portion. Today, with a simple workbench, a few tools, and a burner which uses gas with oxygen or air, this procedure shapes marvelous jewels of glass in a direct manner (see figure 6).

Free-blowing (or offhand blowing) is more difficult, requiring rather elaborate and expensive facilities. This technique was invented around 50 B.C. (glassmaking was already 1500 years old then). The glass is manipulated at the end of a hollow iron pipe (the blowpipe or blowiron), which is about four feet long. Molten glass is made within a refractory container in a furnace, either by remelting marbles or chunks of glass, or by fusing together the raw materials that form glass. The fluid glass is wound upon or "gathered" on the tip of the hollow iron pipe. It is then shaped and manipulated, inflated, tooled, sheared, and spun out or forced in (see figures 7 through 10). More glass can be applied and decorated by various operations (see figure 11).

Figure 6. "Bimorph."

The shape at the end of the iron is maintained at the proper degree of fluidity by reheating periodically in a small furnace called the "glory hole." Great skill and coordination are required to gather, to shape, and to keep the glass from flowing off the iron.

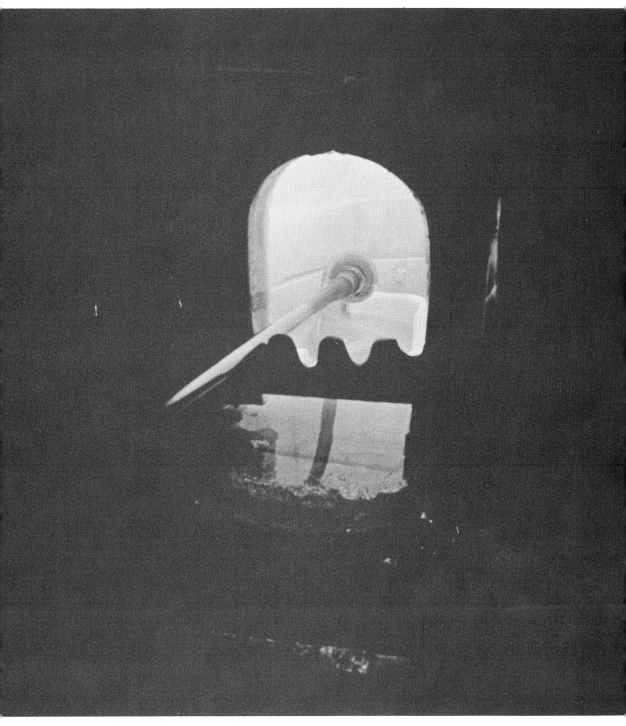

Figure 7. Gathering glass.

Figure 8. Marvering glass, with gathering glass in the background.

Figure 9. Spinning out a disk.

In contrast, the simplicity and low cost of equipment for the flameworker, and the case of acquiring the necessary skill, make flameworking of interest to the college or high school art student, to the craftsman, and to the hobbyist (see figures 12 through 15).

Figure 10. Forcing a disk into a bowl shape.

Figure 11. Vase designed by Lucrecia Mayano de Muniz. (*Glass 1959*)

Figure 12. "Seed Form."

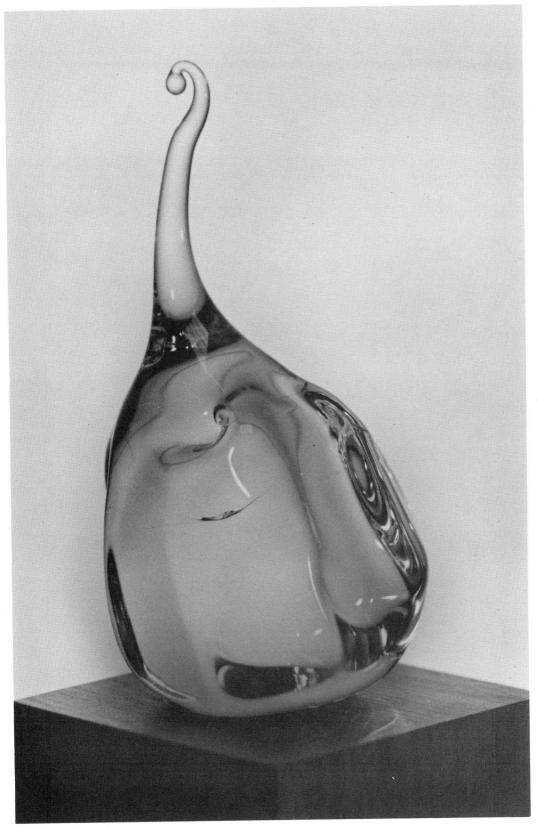

Figure 13. "Fruit."

Figure 14. "Whirling Dervish."

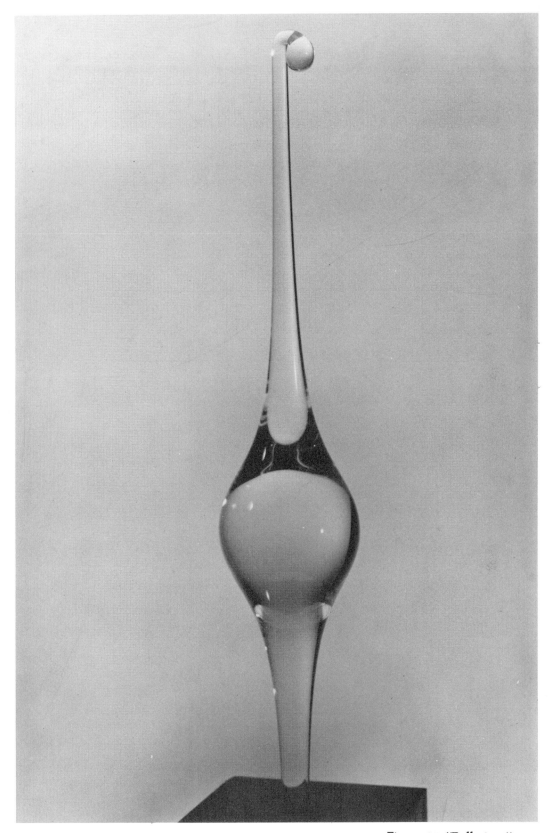

Figure 15. "Ballerina."

3. A Brief History of Flameworking

1650-1800: THE EARLY PERIOD

Robert Hooke, in his *Micrographia*, 1665 (New York: Dover Publications, 1961), describes in great detail his microscopic observations. In the preface he mentions the use of the lamp for flameworking:

"And hence it is, that if you take a very clear piece of a broken Venice Glass, and in a Lamp draw it out into very small hairs or threads, then holding the ends of these threads in the flame, till they melt and run into a small round Globul, or drop, which will hang at the end of the thread . . ."

He then tells of mounting these in wax on a stick, and grinding and polishing them for use as microscopic lenses.

An earlier reference, *Ars Magna Lucis et Umbria* by Althanasius Kircher, 1646, accounts for all the microscopes of his day. It describes tiny spherical lenses along with other shapes. It is reasonable to suppose that some of the minute spherical lenses used in the earliest microscopes in the period 1600-1650 were made by flameworking.

Hooke also mentions making very fine glass tubes, which he calls "pipes," which were "melted in the flame of a lamp." He made thermometers, starting with tubing made in a "Glass-house":

"These I can easily in the flame of a lamp, urged with the blast of a pair of Bellows, seal and close together . . ."

Glass eyes are mentioned as early as 1687, and these were un-

18

doubtedly made by flameworking. This would represent an advance in technical skill over the simple operations described by Hooke.

The earliest illustrations the author has found showing lamp-workers are in the Diderot Encyclopedia of 1768. There the torch is used to make glass pearls, and the foot-bellows is clearly shown.

1800-1880: SCIENTIFIC APPLICATIONS TO CHEMISTRY

The use of lampworking for scientific apparatus increased from 1800-1880. For example, in 1820, De la Rue sealed platinum filaments inside a glass bulb, and evacuated it to make an electric light. By 1862, various designs of glass vacuum pumps were being developed. The Geissler pump led to the Töpler pump and others, all fabricated from glass. Glass vacuum gauges were made in 1872 (the McLeod gauge) and Edison developed his electric light in 1879.

AFTER 1880: THE RISE OF SCIENTIFIC APPLICATIONS TO PHYSICS

A burst of activity in physics after 1880 was made possible by glass blowing using the torch, if only to seal off bulbs after evacuation. The work of Hertz, Crookes, J. J. Thomson, Lenard, Dewar, and others, in various areas of experimental physics, required glass blowing of simple bulbs to complex double- and triple-walled flasks.

This use of glass blowing has continued to the present day in both physics and chemistry. The scientific glass blower is the unheralded aide of the scientist. Without him, scientific advances of many kinds would have been impossible.

During the period around 1880 flameworking techniques were developed to make marvelously realistic botanical and zoological models. The best-known workers were the Bohemians, Leopold Blaschka (1822-1895) and his son Rudolph (1857-1939). Leopold Blaschka's father had been a lampworker also, and Leopold was an apprentice to him, as Rudolph was to Leopold. In 1853, Leopold took a voyage to America, collecting and sketching marine animals. On his return to Bohemia, he made glass models of marine life for the Dresden Natural History Museum.

19

In 1886 Professor George Lincoln Goodale, founder of Harvard's Botanical Museum, persuaded the Blaschkas to make glass flowers for the museum. Later, the project was financed by Mrs. Charles Eliot Ware and her daughter Mary Lee Ware. From 1890 to 1936 the entire output of father and son went to the Ware collection at Harvard.

The collection ultimately reached 847 models in 164 plant families. It went far beyond flowers, and included fruit, fungi, ferns, mosses, lichens, and algae—even a butterfly perched on a bachelor's button. The delicate glass models were shaped and then painted with powdered colored glasses, which were then fused. Upon annealing, they were covered with a special varnish to remove the glassy look. The accuracy is amazing—a great cluster of flowers of the Hercules'-club shows more than 2500 buds and blossoms, each with the exact number of petals and stamens, and each bud perfectly rendered.

1914: THE INTRODUCTION OF BOROSILICATE GLASS

An important step forward was the development and introduction of borosilicate glass. This increased the use of glass in the laboratory and helped to achieve stronger and more chemically durable apparatus. The production of apparatus has gradually moved into the factory, although still using flameworking techniques, at least for assembly from standard machine-made parts. Such techniques have made possible radio tubes, radar and television tubes, and special information-storage tubes for early digital computers (the MIT "Whirlwind," for example). For more specialized work there are custom shops, or a scientific glass blower associated with a research laboratory or university. Laser tubes have come out of such shops. As the parts required have become more complex, new methods of working glass have been developed. The glass-blowing lathe, for example, permits handling large size tubing with perfect alignment and synchronous rotation.

4. The Physical Properties of Glass

The brittleness of glass when cold, its fluidity when very hot, are apparent and well-known properties. But those of surface tension and expansion with increasing temperature are also of importance to the glass worker. The surface tension property causes fluid glass to behave like a liquid. The effect is to round off sharp surfaces and give a smoothness to them. The surfaces become "fire-polished." The expansion-temperature relation, usually called thermal expansion, is a property of glass also common to other rigid materials. As the temperature rises, and before it gets so high that the glass becomes fluid, the piece expands or increases in length. This expansion (or contraction when cooled) can produce a stress between different parts of a single piece of glass, and can cause the glass to crack or fracture. This stress can be reduced by controlled cooling or "annealing." For a more detailed discussion, see Appendices 1 and 2.

Part Two

FORMING BY
FLAMEWORKING

5. Shaping Without Blowing

The operations involved in flameworking are cutting, rotating, bending, pulling, pushing, sealing, blowing, and annealing. In this section we shall exclude blowing and consider working with rod or cane, or sheets or slabs, and building up various shapes by the other operations mentioned above. Thus these shapes might be described as "solid," "monolithic," or "non-hollow," although they can be most complex. For example, they could have bubbles incorporated into the design, or could be very lacy in appearance.

The arrangement of the tools and torch on the glass bench is dictated by convenience. The torch is immediately in front of the worker; tools are placed conveniently to the right (for a right-handed person); glass and pieces just finished can be placed to the left; containers with small rods and bits of glass for handles or for applying decorations are in a can further to the right; the "annealing can" is placed to the right or on the floor.

The description of the torch and its operation and control, with the control of the oxygen tank, will be described in Chapter 6. For a person without experience in the handling of similar equipment, that section should be consulted before starting to work. Of the different types of torches available, only the hand torch is used here. It is mounted in a support, but can be easily detached and held in the hand for certain finishing operations. The torch has an easily adjusted flame size.

BEGINNER'S WARNINGS

1. Be careful in breaking cane or tubing after scratching with a sharp file, or with sheet glass or slabs after scribing with a glass cutter. Properly scratched or scribed, glass will break without much applied pressure.
2. For flameworking, *always* wear Didymium-pink glass-blowing glasses, for protection from the bright yellow light of sodium vapor in the flame. The sodium vapor comes from the sodium oxide volatilized out of the hot glass.
3. Long after glass has lost its red color, it is still too hot to touch.

CUTTING CANE AND SLABS

To cut small cane up to ³/₈ inches diameter, it is first scratched with a sharp triangular file. The scratch is clean and neat, and only a few millimeters long. It is made precisely perpendicular to the

Figure 16. Breaking cane or rod.

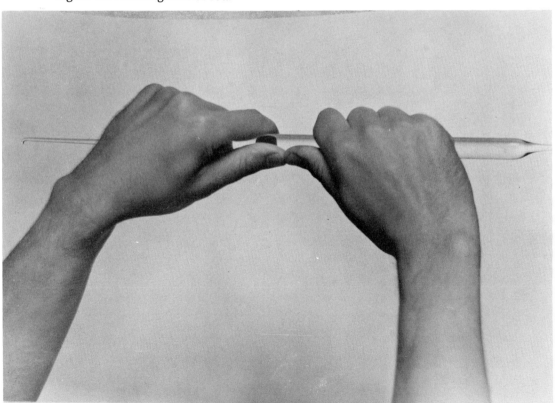

cane. The scratch is then wetted slightly, and the cane is broken by bending and pulling at the same time (see figure 16). Practice on 1/4-inch cane first. If the cane doesn't break immediately and easily, deepen the scribe mark. In parting a four-foot-long cane be sure that the long ends will not swing upon breaking and strike nearby objects. Cane of any size can be flameworked until soft and pulled apart (see later section, "Pulling a Point").

Sheet or slabs can be scribed with the glass cutter's carbide wheel, then broken by tapping with the wooden end of the cutting tool, essentially in the manner in which window glass can be cut. Of course, an expert person "breaks" the scribed window glass by bending and pulling apart at the scribe mark, but the tapping method can do the job. Pieces too thick to cut this way, or of irregular thickness, can be cut on the diamond cut-off saw under a water spray.

CLEANING

Glass should be clean and dry before heating and before sealing pieces together. Usually glass from the supplier is quite clean, and wiping off the dust will be sufficient. Otherwise washing with water and detergent is usually adequate.

PREHEATING

A piece of glass thrust into the hottest part of the torch flame will crack or even fly apart (this is sometimes called "heat shock"). The effect of the local expansion, and consequent stress, depends on the shape of the piece. For example, heating the center of a massive piece is much worse than heating an edge. The cracks formed in a 5/8-inch piece of cane which was heated strongly in the flame are shown in figure 17. A low expansion glass like a borosilicate glass can be heated more rapidly than a high expansion glass (see Appendix 1, section 9).

27

The procedure for preheating glass is first to decrease the oxygen supply to produce a relatively cool, bushy flame. The glass is held out beyond the flame tip, and slowly brought closer, and finally brought into the hot part of the flame. The glass is rotated during

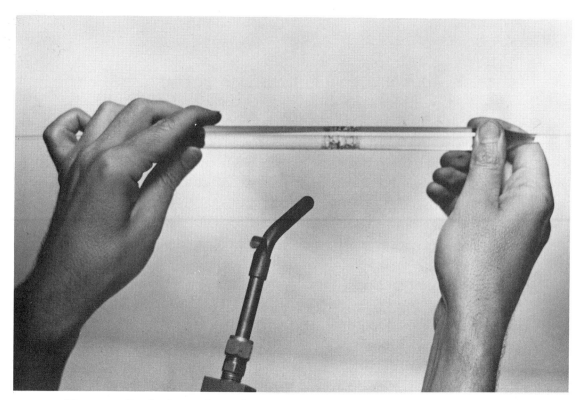

Figure 17. Cracks due to thermal stress.

this operation. At the same time the oxygen valve is controlled periodically to supply more oxygen, making a smaller and hotter flame.

To a certain extent this process is a trial and error process, to avoid wasting time with needless preheating. Thus you speed up the steps until you have a failure, and then back off, taking a little more time. Naturally, for assembling an elaborate piece, work more carefully so as to avoid a crack which will be difficult to reseal.

BURNER ADJUSTMENT

The size of the flame should be varied according to the size of the piece or the particular operation involved. Furthermore, the temperature of the flame should be varied. With increasing skill, higher flame temperatures can be used with faster working speed. However, an excessively hot flame will volatilize some of the constituents of the glass, changing its properties or producing bubbles. With too low a flame temperature and prolonged working of the glass, some crystallization can take place. This is called "devitrifi-

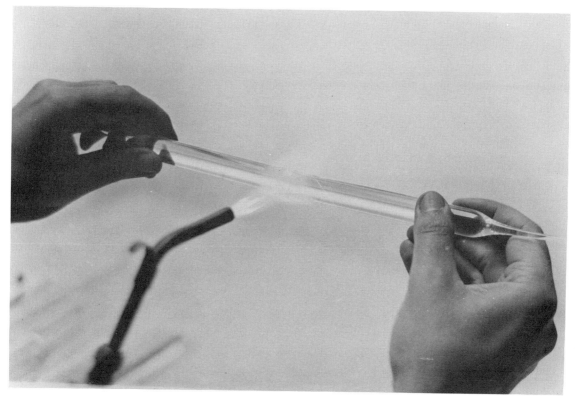

Figure 18. Holding glass.

cation." Reheating in a hotter flame will usually correct this condition.

THE POSITION OF THE HANDS

The left hand, palm down, holds most of the weight of the glass. The fingers take a position on the cane so as to balance the left section of the glass when the part in the flame is fluid. The right hand holds the lighter, shorter section. The right hand is palm up, and the glass is held in the fingers. The glass is rotated smoothly to maintain the fluid portion concentric with the axis of the cane. The top surface is rotated away from the worker. The position of the hands and direction of rotation are shown in figure 18.

29

THE ROTATION OF THE WORK

The most fundamental operation in flameworking is rotation of the work. This is certainly the case with cane or tubing, where it is necessary to have a section uniformly fluid, and to have gravity act on that section in a symmetrical manner. Of course, after a complex shape has been formed, rotation or turning may be done in an irregular manner, or the heating may be done locally or in some asymmetric manner.

An additional reason for rotation is that the lower surfaces of the glass cool more rapidly than the upper surfaces. Thus rotation evens the cooling rate, and should be continued even after removing the glass from the flame. Good coordination of the hands is required or the fluid section will become distorted in a manner other than that intended; that is, twisted, misaligned, pushed, or pulled, although each of these actions may be desired at some time.

A simple way to practice is to connect two pieces of cane with a narrow piece of cloth or sticky tape having about the same diameter as the cane. The beginner should use the same position as in figure 18 and rotate the canes and cloth uniformly, without twisting, misaligning, pushing, or pulling.

The work is controlled by the thumbs and forefingers, with the other fingers aiding slightly, and the palm of the left hand serving as a slight support. The movements must be coordinated, even though canes of different diameters may be held in each hand—the movements are synchronized. Each turning motion is about 45°, so in the strictest sense the movements are not truly uniform, but a series of angular motions. As mentioned above, the left hand holds the greatest weight, and the right hand has the more delicate job of keeping perfectly coordinated with the left.

BEGINNER'S WORK

Here are some simple things for the beginner to try so that he gets a "feel" for glass as it gets fluid.

30

1. Pulling glass *in the flame:* preheat, heat a section with rotation, then pull out the glass while keeping it in the flame. The glass stays hot, and the thin section gets very thin quickly, and then pulls apart. Repeat this several times.

2. Pulling glass *out of the flame:* preheat, heat a section with rotation, remove from the flame (lift above the flame) and pull the two

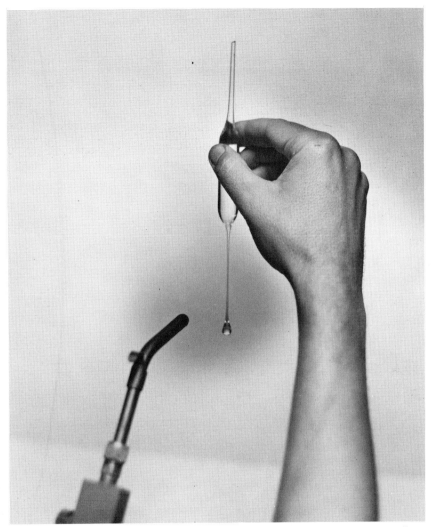

Figure 19. Surface tension effect.

ends. As the glass cools, the thin section cools most quickly and gets rigid. Glass will continue to be pulled out of the hotter sections where the cane is thicker. Repeat, pulling very quickly, then more and more slowly. Try this many times to get the "feel" for the starting temperature (orange-red in color for the borosilicate glass) and fluidity and behavior as you pull. Try to control the diameter of the thin section just as you desire.

3. After pulling, hold steady until cool. Also twist ends after pulling so as to see how long it takes the glass to become rigid, and what section remains fluid longest.

4. "Experiments" on surface tension: heat the end of a pulled-out point from the above work, holding it vertically down in the

31

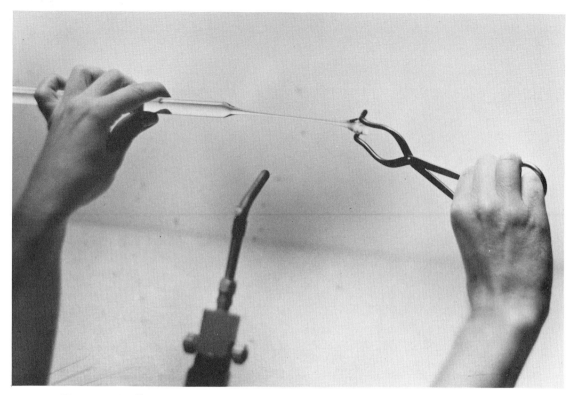

Figure 20. Pulling a point.

flame, as shown in figure 19. Watch how the glass "pulls up" into a rounded ball, and then how it can get large enough and heavy enough to fall under its own weight.

5. An operation related to heating a rod and keeping the fluid center under control is that of heating the ends of two rods at the same time in the flame. They are rotated uniformly, taking care not to touch them together, until both tips are about the same color. Then the ends are pressed together up above the flame. The sealed section is then heated with rotation and pushed together, then pulled out slightly until smooth and uniform in diameter.

PULLING A POINT

"Pulling a point" is the simple operation of heating the cane and pulling out a thinner section, while holding it out of the flame. The thin section should be about 3/16 inch in diameter, and strong enough to serve as a handle. In this case it should be about 4 inches long, so that the hand can be away from the heat of the flame (see

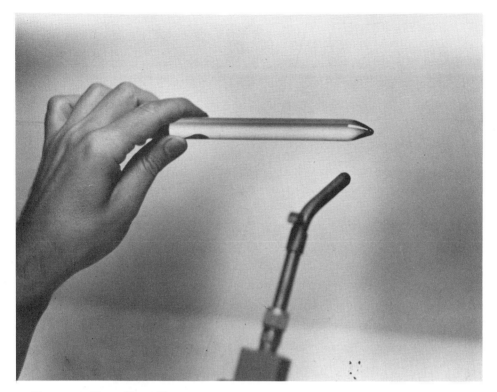

Figure 21. Rounding off a cane.

figure 20). In addition to serving as a handle, the point is also a narrowing of the cane, a preliminary step to "rounding off" the cane. To round off the cane, the point is heated close to where the glass thins down, and then pulled off in the flame. This end may have to be reheated and pulled off a second time so that only a very small point is left, which is heated strongly so that the glass rounds over (see figure 21).

THICKENING A ROD

"Thickening" a rod or cane is another basic operation for building up a complex shape. The glass is heated strongly, with rotation, about $1/2$ inch in from where it starts to narrow to the point. It could be heated elsewhere, but the steps here are described to follow the pulling of the point above, where the point not only serves as a handle but will eventually be removed and the end rounded off. After heating strongly, the glass is simply pushed together, with stepwise rotation between pushes. It bulges out and thickens as shown in

33

figure 22. The glass is heated strongly about $^3/_8$ inch away, and more glass is pushed into the bulge. The process is continued, moving down the rod. The beginner should try to build up a single bulge as large as possible, and also try to thicken a rod for as long a distance as possible, with relatively uniform diameter.

ACCESSORY TOOLS

The accessory tools are very simple. The basic set for shaping cane is: forceps (preferably with wooden handles), tongs, blocks of smooth carbon, a carbon paddle, and glass cane of small diameter (3/16 inch or $^1/_4$ inch) to be attached in various places for handles or to serve as material to be applied, depending upon the design. Other tools can be invented or adapted as required.

BUILDING UP A COMPLEX SHAPE

The steps to building up a complex shape will now be described along with the use of the tools mentioned above. This shape will start out being sufficiently general—and not necessarily an interesting

Figure 22. Thickening a rod.

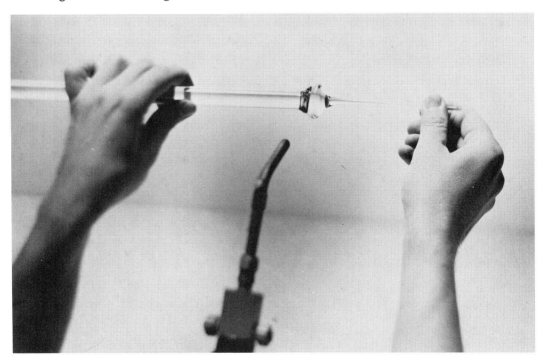

Sprouting Seed

Sprouting Seed

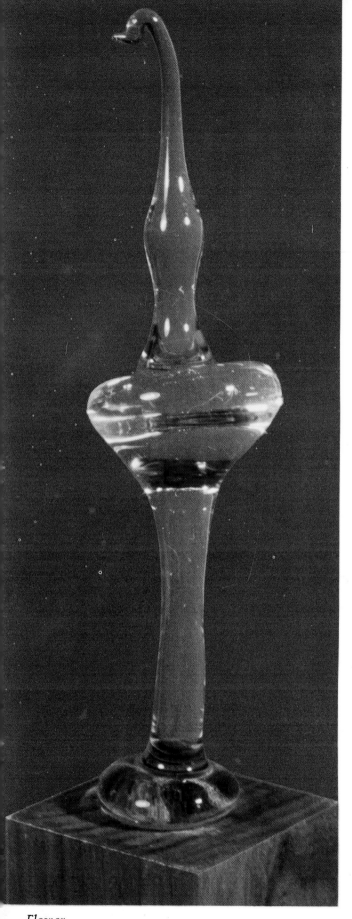

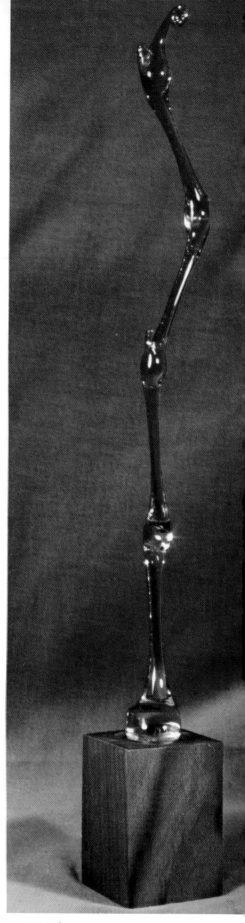

Flower

Weed

Stone #1

Stones

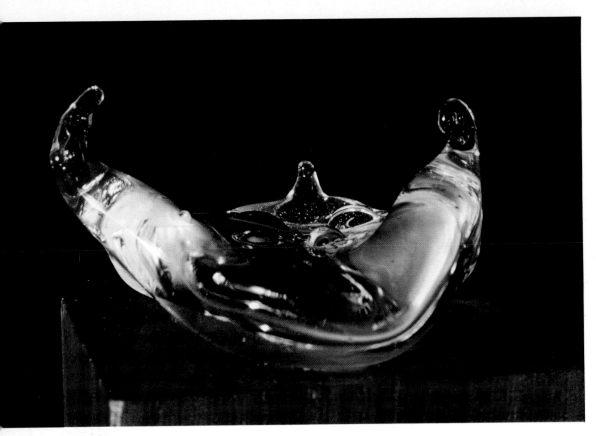

Beach Stone

Seed Form

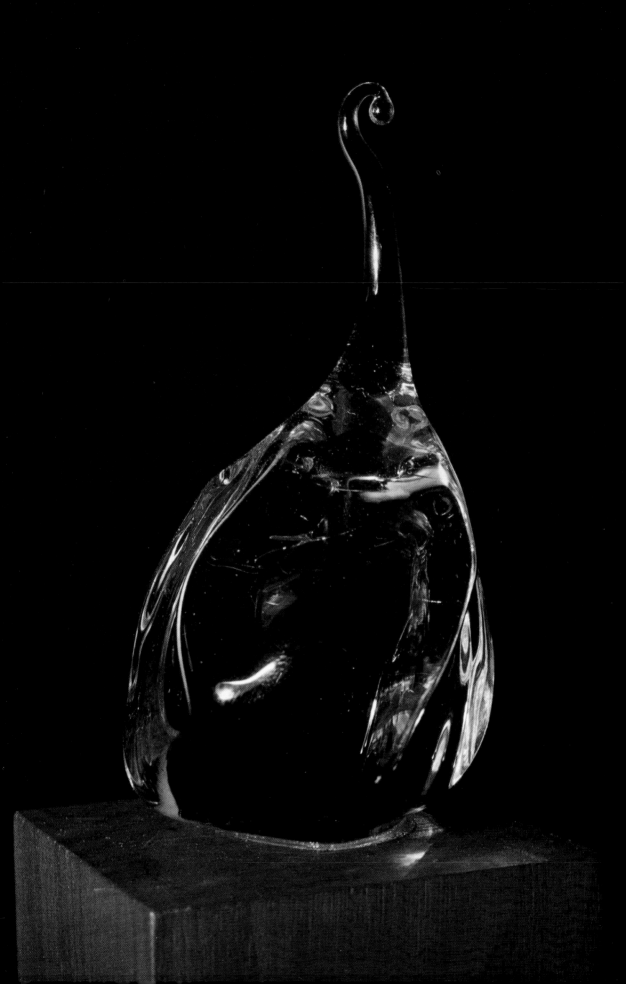

Philosopher's Stones

Fruit

Philosopher's Stones "Introverted"

sculpture—so the beginner can then modify it into something he likes, using parts or all of the procedure described.

A glass cane of ⅝-inch diameter is chosen. This cane is about 4 feet long, as supplied.

1. Wipe the glass clean.

2. Heat the cane about 12 inches from one end. Heat it gently, by holding it out beyond the torch flame, and gradually moving it in (as described under "Preheating"). The right hand holds the glass six inches in from that end, and the left at the "balance point," 1½ feet in from the other end (if the cane is four feet long).

3. The glass is rotated, and then a point is pulled out, slowly, with the glass above the flame. Try to get the thin section 8 to 12 inches long and almost 3/16 inch in diameter. It is allowed to cool for a few seconds (hold taut, so there is no bending) until rigid, and then the center of the thin section is heated and the glass pulled apart in the flame.

4. The ends may have to be rounded up in the flame to be made safe to handle.

At this stage the beginner has simply repeated the operation of pulling a point.

5. The section held in the right hand is laid down, with the hot end on a carbon block.

6. After the point on the long section is cool enough to handle, the point is held in the right hand, a new "balance point" is located for the left hand, and the process of pulling a point about twelve inches from the right end is repeated. Thus four pieces are prepared for future work from the original piece. Each one is laid down in order so that the coolest piece can now be picked up.

The beginner is now ready for the next step.

7. The first piece prepared is picked up and with the point in the right hand and the rod in the left, the operation of thickening a section is carried out. This process is repeated and a series of thickened sections are then built up (see figures 23 and 24).

The beginner is now at the stage described earlier under thickening a rod.

8. At the end of the last thickened bulge, the cane is heated strongly and pulled out slightly to thin down (see figure 25).

35

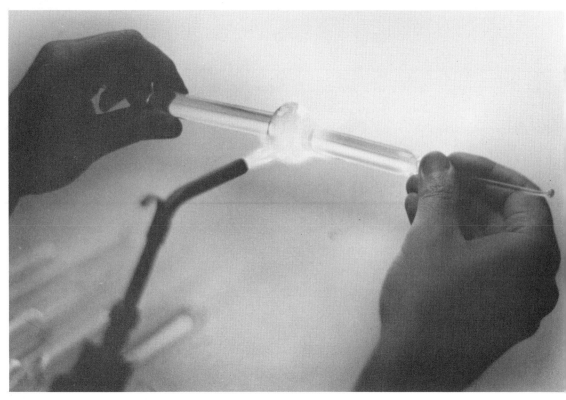

Figure 23. Thickening a rod: 1st section.

Figure 24. Thickening a rod: 2nd section.

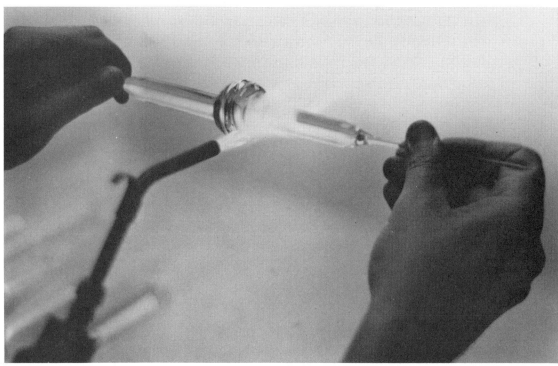

Figure 25. Pulling out to thin down.

The beginner is now ready to remove this end, as neatly as possible, with the plan to flatten it for a base. These steps will now be described.

9. The thinned section is heated and pulled off. The knob is heated, and the excess glass is removed by touching it with a small cane and pulling out, or by seizing it with the forceps and pulling out. The forceps tends to chill the knob, so that the pulling must be done quickly.

10. Now the end is heated and pressed against a carbon block to flatten it for a base (see figure 26). Of course, it is held by the point at the other end.

11. The pressed end is chilled when it touches the carbon, and has a slightly roughened surface. It is reheated to smooth over.

The object now has a base, which was made at one end, although it might have been put on the side instead. The object is ready for application of more glass: knobs, lumps, or small curling rods like branches.

12. Heat small canes quite hot, and the object less hot, but with the object in the left hand (held by the point) and the canes in the

37

Figure 26. Flattening glass for a base.

right. Be careful not to touch them together accidentally as they will stick together. Try different size rods and different methods of heating. An alternate procedure is to heat one spot on the object very hot and pull some glass out by touching it with a cooler cane. Examples are shown in figures 27 through 30.

13. Work on these decorative applications with the torch, fusing down, heating the very tip (you may have to set the object on its base and hand hold the torch) and pull out more glass.

Figure 27. Carbon deposit after flame annealing.

Figure 28.
Glass in annealing can, partially covered.

Figure 29. Heating a thin section.

40 The object is now ready for finishing, which involves removing the point. It may be more convenient to anneal first, and then after the object is cool to work on the tip with a very small flame (this procedure was followed here).

14. "Flame anneal" and transfer to the simple annealing can. This is described in detail in Chapter 22. (See figures 27 and 28.)

Figure 30. Pulling to separate.

15. When cool, place the object on its base, and hold the torch in
    the right hand and the point in the left. Heat the point where you
    want it to end, and when the glass gets soft, pull up, or bend it
    into a gently curving form. Then heat a section hot and separate
    it in the flame. Round up the slender end if you desire (see figures
    29, 30, and 31).

Figure 31. Heating tip to finish.

FIRST SCULPTURE: "PHILOSOPHER'S STONE"

The following operations are used to make a "Philosopher's Stone." They may be repeated so that many "stones" can be made and then arranged in patterns to make a decorative little sculpture. Three or five or more can be arranged and cemented to a wooden block with a transparent epoxy (see figures 32 and 33).

1. Take a four-foot rod of $5/8$-inch glass and pull a point about 12 inches from the end. Separate to leave a handle.

2. After the handle is cool enough to hold, heat the glass (point in right hand, main section in left) about $1/2$ inch in from where it narrows to the point and push together to make a bulge. Heating to the left of the bulge, push in more glass until the basic shape is formed (see figure 34).

3. Let it cool somewhat, then heat close to the bulge (to the left) and pull out a point there (see figure 35). Heat to pull off, and clean up by heating and touching with a rod, pulling off excess glass, or use the forceps and pull off.

42

Figure 32. "Philosopher's Stones." (Introverted)

Figure 33. "Philosopher's Stones." (Extroverted)

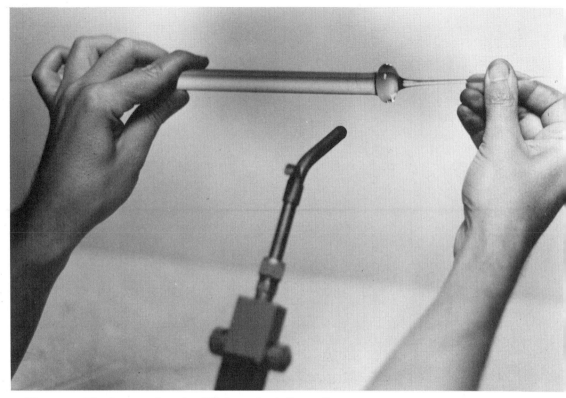

Figure 34. Thickening glass for "Philosopher's Stone."

Figure 35. Separating the Stone.

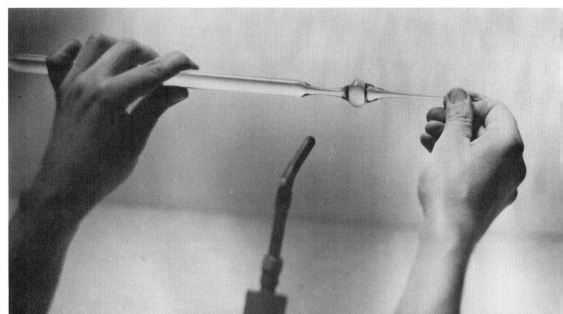

Figure 36. Flattening the base.

Figure 37. Rounding off the tip of the Stone.

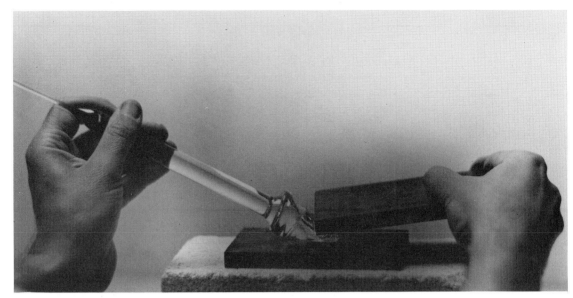

Figure 38. Flattening a thickened section for "Beach Stone."

4. Heat knob, and press flat on carbon for the base of the "stone," using the point for a handle (hold that in the right hand); (see figure 36).
5. Hold vertically, rest glass on its base on the carbon block, pick up the torch in the right hand and heat the point, pulling it off with the left hand. Heat gently for the small tip to round off and bend slightly.

THREE EXAMPLES: "BEACH STONE," "SEA CREATURE," "SPROUTING SEED"

The operations or steps for making each of these examples are those already described with perhaps slight variations, except for the "Beach Stone." For the "Beach Stone" the most desirable starting material would be an irregular slab of glass. However, it can be made from cane and the process will be described starting with cane in order to illustrate another sequence of operations.

46

"Beach Stone"

1. Start with 5/8-inch cane and thicken a section.
2. Flatten it with the carbon paddle on another piece of carbon. Flatten only a small section at a time (the glass becomes chilled) and reheat, flattening more. Thicken more and flatten (see figure 38).

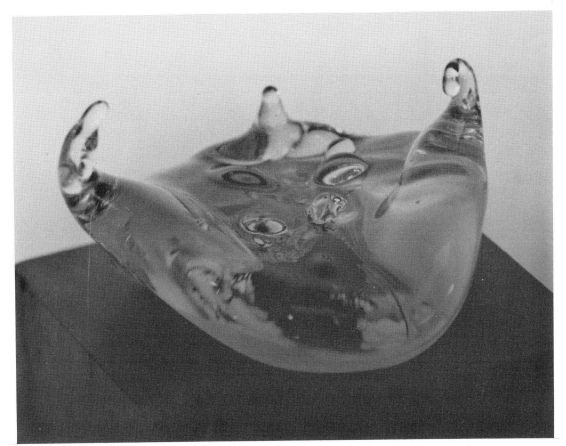

Figure 39. "Beach Stone." (Finished)

3. Continue with the shaping, adding more glass, pulling and twisting, applying lumps and little nodules, removing handles, heating and flattening part for the base.
4. Placing the "stone" on the carbon, holding the last handle in the left hand, pick up the torch in the right and flame off the handle.
5. The finished "stone" (see figure 39) is flame-annealed and transferred to the simple annealing can.

"Sea Creature"

This sculpture is related in procedure to the basic shape described under "Complex Shape" above. Here, after a cane has been thickened, it is curved slightly and flattened on the "side" for the base. Finally, the last handle is removed. The steps are shown in figures 40 to 42.

"Sprouting Seed"

This is a very simple sculpture related to the "Philosopher's Stone." The steps are shown in figures 43 and 44.

47

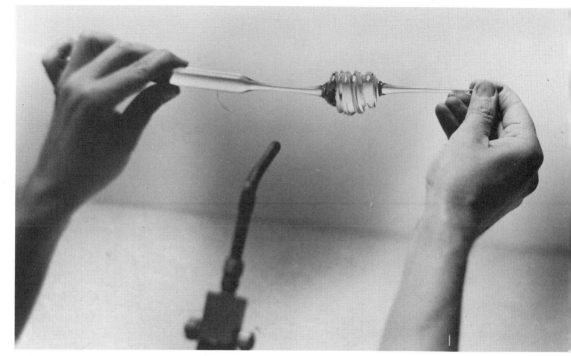

Figure 40. Thickening a cane for "Sea Creature."

Figure 41. Flattening a shape on the side.

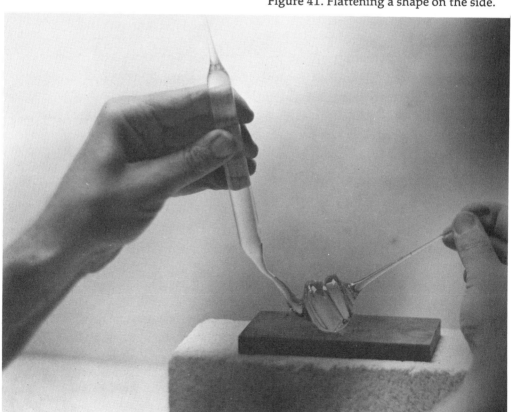

Figure 42. "Sea Creature." (Finished)

Following these examples, the beginner is now prepared to make any of his own designs consistent with the above methods, or he can invent his own variations. The variety of shapes and forms, small and compact or large and intertwined, is so great that they could never be enumerated. Even a very simple shape—a teardrop—can be elongated or squat, have a variety of tip shapes, have bits of applied glass, and many other design possibilities. Some beginners might like to have more specific suggestions, and therefore another set of examples has been assembled. These are based on plant and animal shapes, but simplified and abstracted. Some have lens-like shapes with especially interesting optical effects.

THE CONSTRUCTION OF ABSTRACT PLANTS AND CREATURES: "ANTEATER," "KIWI," "SHORE BIRD," "PLANT," "CYMBIDIUM"

The steps to form the first three shapes evolve out of the "Sprouting Seed," if one begins with cane. Small discs of glass would furnish a simpler starting point, but the process will be described using cane to show the evolution of designs.

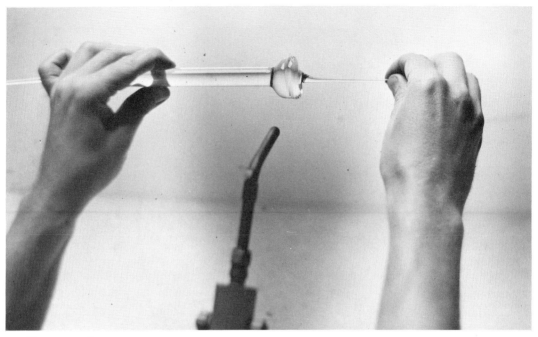

Figure 43. Starting "Sprouting Seed."

Figure 44. "Sprouting Seed." (Finished)

Figure 45. Making a lens shape.

"Anteater," "Kiwi," and "Shore Bird"

1. Start with ⁵⁄₈-inch cane and thicken a section, pushing three or four heated areas together.
2. Pull a point and round off at one end.
3. Heat strongly and flatten on carbon, reheating and flattening, with a slight rolling or rounding motion, to make one half of a lens (concave) shape.
4. Attach a ⁵⁄₈-inch rod to what will become the edge of the lens, anticipating that this rod will later become the head of each of the creatures.
5. Pull off the other point, and round that off.
6. Heat strongly and flatten this other side of the lens, reheating and rounding the surface.
7. Reheat, and permit rounding to take place by surface tension.
8. Attach another rod for the tail.
9. Heat and pull out the head.
10. Apply small bits of glass, using fine canes, for the feet and for the eyes. Flatten at the feet for a base.

51

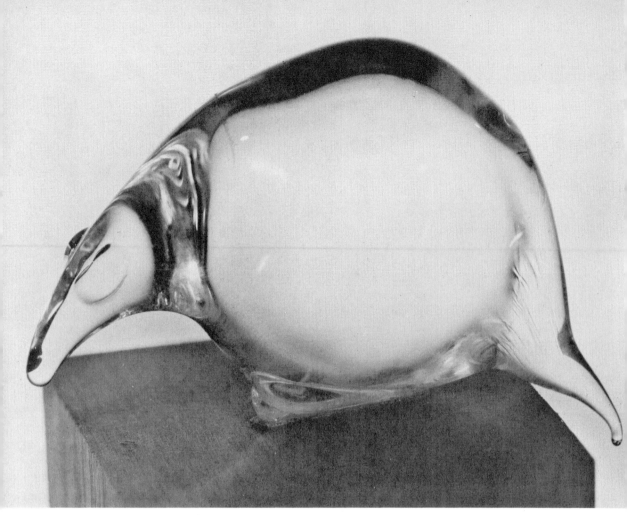

Figure 46. "Anteater."

11. Heat, and pull out the tail, according to the design.
12. Separate one handle, either the head or the tail.
13. Flame-anneal, and place in the annealing can.
14. When cool use a very small flame and separate the other handle, as the object rests on its base on the carbon block.

"Plant" and "Cymbidium"

1. Start with ⅝-inch cane, thicken a section for a base for the "Plant."

2. Heat and pull out to give thinner sections, separated by bulbs or joints of the plant. Keep repeating and pulling out, very straight, three or four sections.
3. Heat with a very fine flame at the joint, and bend slightly.
4. For the "Plant," apply small bits of glass, using fine canes and then

pulling off. These small attached sections are heated and allowed to curl over, for small leaves.

5. Flower parts for the "Cymbidium" are made separately (actually they should be made before one starts the main stem) by flattening a section of cane and pulling out, reheating the thinner, flat part with a small flame, and pulling out a tapered section. These are then "flame cut" and can later be picked up with tweezers and applied.

6. The flower parts for the "Cymbidium" are attached, using a very small flame.

Figure 47. "Kiwi."

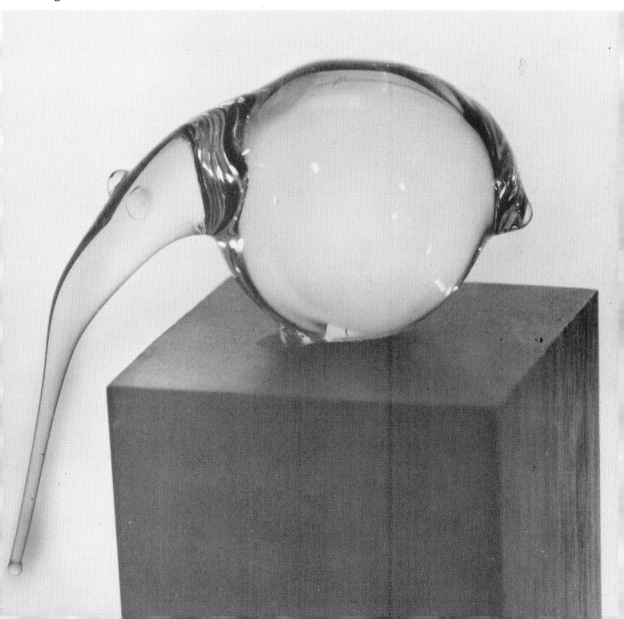

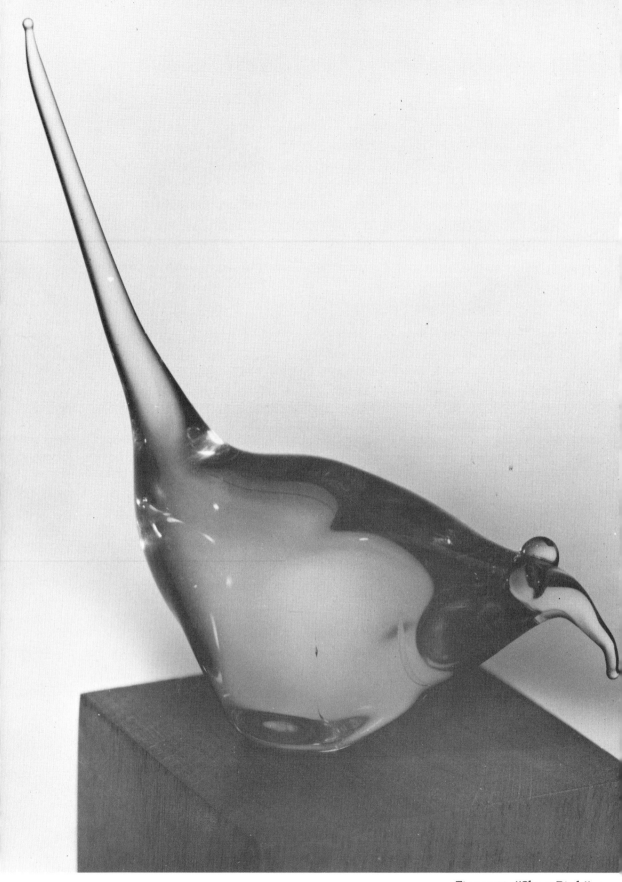

Figure 48. "Shore Bird."

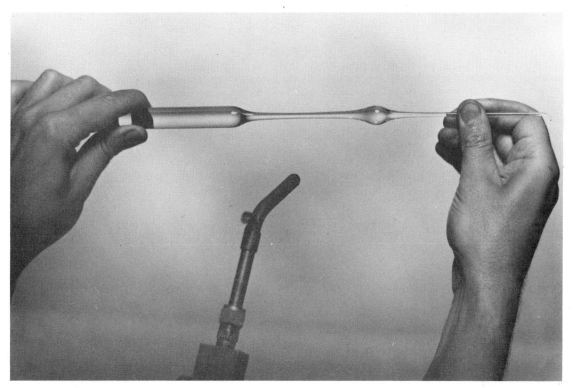

Figure 49. Making joints for "Plant."

7. When the "Plant" is cool, it can be held between a joint, and the rod next to the base pulled off. Then the end is rounded off and pressed flat on the carbon.

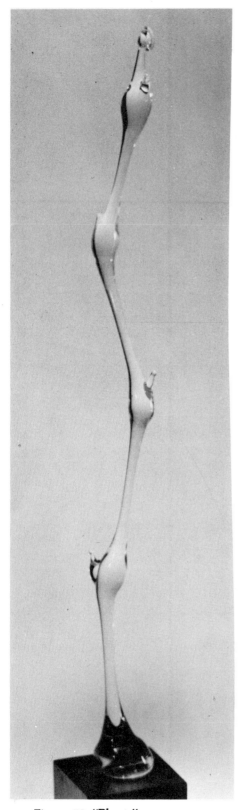

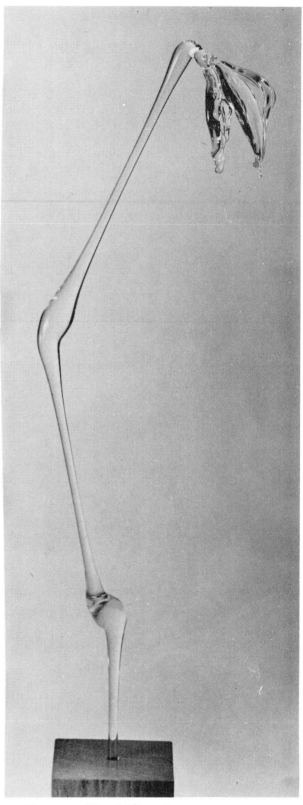

Figure 50. "Plant."　　　　　　　　Figure 51. "Cymbidium."

6. Shaping by Blowing Techniques

In the preceding section, all techniques which involve blowing into the glass were carefully avoided. The beginner was introduced to a series of operations leading finally to making a generalized shape, which involved all of the operations. A first sculpture was described, the "Philosopher's Stone," and then three examples. The beginner could have gone on his own, creating his own shapes and inventing modifications of procedures or new techniques, giving his fantasy free reign. Or he could have looked at other examples, the shapes based on abstractions of animals and plants, and following that, invented his own designs.

In this section the use of hollow glass, starting with tubing, will be described. The new operation of blowing will be of major importance. Following the procedure of the last section, various operations will be described (there will be some repetition) and these will lead to the construction of a generalized shape. Then four specific examples will be described.

CUTTING TUBES AND BOTTLES 57

To cut small glass tubing (up to ½-inch diameter), the procedure is like that for cutting cane. The tubing is scratched with a sharp triangular file (one checks the file visually to locate a section which has not been dulled). The scratch is clean and neat, only a few millimeters long, and perpendicular to the tubing. The scratch is then wetted slightly, and the tubing broken by bending and pulling at the same time. As with the cane, it takes confidence and precise bending and pulling, and if the tubing doesn't break immediately and easily, one can scribe mark again in the same place (so as not to get two marks). As with the cane, watch out that the ends of long rods do not strike some object close by when the glass separates. Larger tubing may be broken, after being scratched with the file, by applying to the end of the scratch mark the tip of a small piece of cane glass made very hot in the flame. The sudden heating produces a crack from the local expansion and stress) which propagates out from the file mark. The crack may encircle the tubing completely. If not, the process is repeated by applying the cane (after reheating) to the glass just ahead of the crack.

Tubing or bottles several inches or more in diameter are cut by a "hot-wire" technique. A scratch is made with the file running completely around the glass (some kind of a guide is made to aid in making the file mark straight). A Nichrome wire heater is used. The wire is looped around the glass precisely over the file mark, but with the ends not touching (for then they would "short out"). The ends are held in clamps, conveniently mounted on wooden handles. The clamps are connected to leads which go to a switch and a resistance. Wire sizes that are adequate are Gauge No. 22 or 24, American Wire Gauge (AWG), formerly Brown and Sharpe Gauge (B and S). The diameters are 25.3 mils and 20.1 mils, respectively. For 12 inches of the No. 22, the room temperature electrical resistance is about 1 ohm. This means that a suitable resistance must be in series with the heating wire, when 110 volts is used. Such resistances are available commercially, as Variacs or Powerstats.

The electric current heats the wire to a red heat for a few seconds. Water is then quickly applied to the heated scratch mark with a pad of wet tissue or cotton. This procedure should produce a clean crack which encircles the glass (watch out for one piece falling off). Irregularities may be removed by softening in the flame and pulling off with the forceps, or by grinding on a lap or a brass plate with wet silicon carbide abrasive.

As with the cane, the glass should be cleaned. It may be clean from the supplier, but dust can be wiped off, inside and outside. If dirty, it should be washed and wiped dry. For small tubing, a wad of cotton can be pushed through it with a metal rod or a smaller cane (be careful not to bend and break the smaller cane!).

PREHEATING

As with the cane, a piece of tubing requires preheating to prevent cracking. A small size tubing, say 1/4-inch diameter, can be thrust almost directly into the flame, but large tubing or bottles present a surface to the flame which, in a sense, is like a flat sheet. If one applies the flame to the center of a flat sheet, that part will expand, set up stresses, and the piece might break explosively. Thus one attempts to heat gradually but over a region around the area to be worked. If possible, a ring-like zone around the tubing should be preheated. The tubing is rotated out beyond the torch flame, brought in gradually, and the flame changed from bushy to more intense by increasing the oxygen. Then the glass is heated in a spot, or a ring, depending on what operation is to follow. As with the cane, the beginner must experiment in decreasing the time of preheating, without breaking the glass, as that time is not really productive.

THE ROTATION OF THE WORK

In working with tubing, as with cane, rotation of the work is the most fundamental operation in lampworking. In general, one will work with larger diameter tubing than with cane, so that it is a little more difficult to hold. Further, many of the sculpture pieces produced from the cane have interesting little imperfections as a result of slight misalignment or twisting, while such misalignment may appear less desirable in the case of tubing. Good coordination of the hands is required—the beginner can practice with two tubes connected with a piece of cloth. In particular, he should work with two different size tubes. He must anticipate the balance point of each section after the center is fluid and position his hands accordingly. The left hand holds the greatest weight, and the right hand provides the coordination of rotation and maintains alignment.

59

BENDING TUBING

It is more difficult to bend tubing without introducing imperfections of folds or flattening than with bending cane. As a prerequisite for a good bend, it is desirable to heat uniformly a length of tubing which is several diameters. For this purpose cross fires or ribbon burners are better than the small torch. However, in using the small torch, the tubing can be held at an angle across the flame, rotated, and moved back and forth in the flame until uniformly soft along a length of several diameters. Upon removal from the flame, it is bent to the desired angle with the bend down (see figure 52). Imperfections occur in tubing upon bending, most often in large tubes and in very small tubes. These imperfections can be worked out by local heating with small flame, so that the form of the bend is maintained by the more rigid rear side of the glass. If the outside tended to be flattened, it can be corrected by blowing while that portion is soft. If the inside had folds, it can be corrected by local heating with a small flame, and alternately shrinking and blowing until it is uniform.

SHRINKING

Shrinking of tubing makes use of the surface tension property, for as glass is a liquid when softened, it tends to deform in such a way as to decrease the total surface. Thus, if the end of a tube is heated it will round over, thicken, and with continued heating even seal across (see figure 53). Likewise, heating in the center with precise alignment of each section will cause the center to shrink in—it can even shrink enough to seal off. Of course such shrinking can be counteracted by blowing or spinning out with a forceps or spinning tools.

60   PULLING A POINT

As with the cane, "pulling a point" is an operation of heating the end of the tubing and drawing it out as shown in figure 54. The point may serve as a handle for rotation or, with the squashed tip removed, it may serve as a mouthpiece for blowing. One scratches

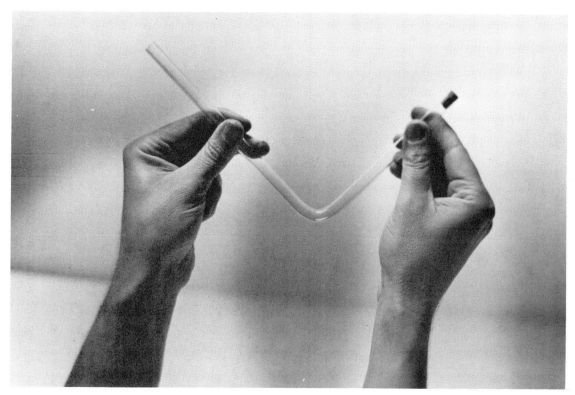

Figure 52. Bending tubing.

Figure 53. Shrinking tubing.

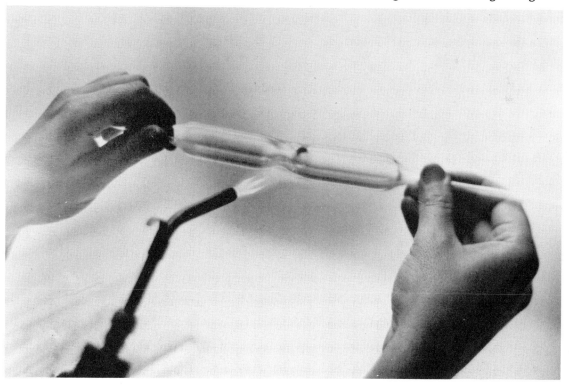

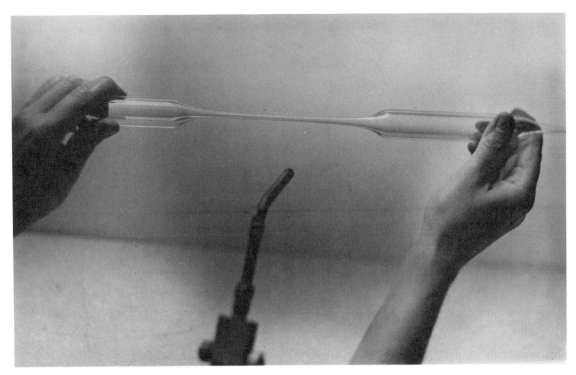

Figure 54. Pulling a point.

Figure 55. Making a seal: 1st step.

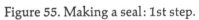

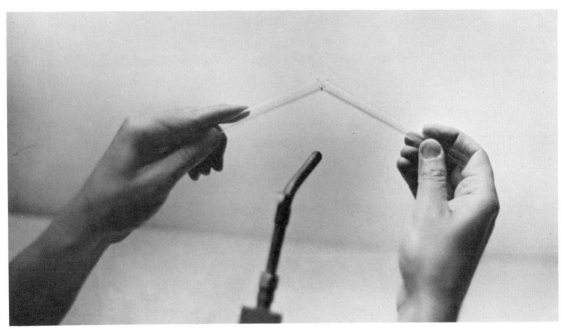

the fine tubing lightly with the triangular file and breaks it (when cool enough to touch) and then fire polishes the new end (wait until cool before putting into the mouth).

Pulling a point is a preliminary operation for closing off a tube. The point is sealed off using a sharp flame. Then the neck is shrunk in order to build up a uniform wall thickness of glass. It is sealed off, excess glass is removed by touching the hot glass with a rod and pulling out, the end is thickened in the flame, and then blown out to a smooth hemisphere.

CUTTING A TUBE IN THE FLAME

To "cut" a tube in the flame one must use some of the previously described operations followed by a blowing operation. For practicing, the complete steps will be described:
1. Pull a point.
2. Remove excess glass by heating and touching a cane, pulling out in the flame.
3. Heat end strongly (it shrinks back almost flat).
4. Blow into the other end (use a swivel joint and rubber tubing if necessary). Blow with a strong puff to make a large, very thin-walled shape, something like a potato.
5. Strike this thin wall with a file or forceps, knocking it off, and even up the edges some.
6. Heat the edges to thicken them to the same wall thickness as the rest of the tubing (they shrink inwards).
7. Heat, spin out with forceps, tapered carbon, or metal triangular tool.

MAKING SEALS

The beginner can practice sealing two tubes of the same diameter. He can cut the tubing, seal together, let cool, cut close to the first seal, and repeat the process so that one piece of 18-inch-long glass might have 12 seals. The procedure is as follows:
1. Cut the tubing as described earlier.
2. Plug the portion to be held in the left hand with a tight fitting cork.
3. Hold tubes in each hand, and heat simultaneously the ends to be

63

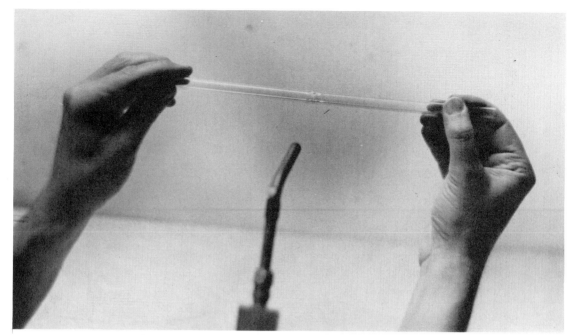

Figure 56. Making a seal: 2nd step.

sealed, with rotation, and to roughly the same temperature. Take care not to touch them together accidentally.

4. When the glass has started to soften and round over slightly, lift above the flame, press together, making the first contact at an angle, then bring them up together in a straight line (see figure 55).

5. Press together slightly, heat, and rotate so that the glass shrinks in a bit.

6. Blow in open end until wall thickness is uniform, with slight bulging, and then pull out at once to uniform diameter, straightening or maintaining alignment (see figure 56).

Other types of seals are with different sizes of tubing, or at right angles to each other (or at some other angle) with either the same size tubes or two different sizes. The surface tension property is such that a hole in the side of a large tube will tend to open up, while heating the end of a small tube tends to close it. Thus it is necessary to anticipate these changes, and prepare the tubes properly for sealing. Otherwise, at the last moment when you are about to contact the glass surfaces, you will discover that they no longer fit together. It is then difficult to move a partially sealed tube slightly to touch and seal over a gap.

Basically, the procedure is to blow out the tubing, after heating in a spot. A small bulb is blown out, heated to shrink back, and repeated, so as to form a short section of tubing. The center is heated strongly and a thin-walled bulb is blown out, cracked off with a file, and the edges cleaned up a bit. The edges are heated and permitted to shrink back to build up the short section of tubing a little more. The whole process is to form an opening of the same size as the piece to be sealed. The end of that piece of tubing and the edges of the opening are heated simultaneously. If there are three open ends (in addition to those two to be sealed), two of them are plugged with corks, leaving the one open that will be most convenient to use as a mouthpiece. The seal is made, first contacting at an angle, then swinging up immediately to touch everywhere, pressing in slightly. The joint is heated all around; then blow into the open tube. This stretches the glass slightly to a uniform wall thickness, with a slight bulging. Pull slightly immediately, stretching the glass so it returns to the proper diameter.

If several tubes are sealed on, then it becomes increasingly difficult to hand-hold both pieces and rotate and heat. The more complex or heavier piece is clamped onto a frame and the torch held in one hand and the simpler or lighter piece in the other. Then the torch is moved slightly to heat both parts. A swivel joint and rubber tubing are used to simplify blowing.

BLOWING

The purpose of this whole section is to make use of blowing in different ways, from using it as an aid to sealing tubes together to blowing hollow shapes or bulbs. It is rather difficult to make large bulbs, more than two inches in diameter. You may start with commercial bulbs, but for our purposes *heavy-walled tubing* is the best starting point. The final bulb will be very thin-walled, and such delicate thinness is in itself of interest artistically.

For making a spherical bulb at the end of the tubing, the first operation is to pull a point, remove excess glass, and heat and rotate to build up a wall of uniform thickness. As the glass collects, it is alternately blown out and permitted to shrink back until more glass has collected. That glass is then heated uniformly.

65

Upon removal from the flame, the work is rotated for a few seconds about the horizontal axis, and then blown into, using a swivel joint if necessary. The blowing is first gentle, then harder as the glass stiffens. The work is rotated continuously. However, if the bulb starts to be non-spherical, because one section expands more than another, that portion is turned down to cool and restrict its expansion, as the underside cools more rapidly.

It may be of interest to develop asymmetry or non-spherical shapes. A rod can be attached to the end for a handle, and during the blowing process can be pulled to elongate the bulb, or pushed in to flatten it. That rod has to be removed later, and the end can be heated and flattened for a base. Or during the blowing process, if rotation is stopped, the cooling will be non-uniform and the shape will tend to be non-spherical (with variation in wall thickness).

As heavy-walled tubing has been used, the thin-walled bulb will be attached to a heavy-walled neck. This neck can be heated close to the bulb and pulled out if a handle has been attached first. Then the handle is removed, and the neck cut off at the desired place, scratching with the triangular file and breaking as described earlier. This neck can be finished by adding a ring of glass, or heating to fire-polish.

If glass had been applied in various ways to the starting tubing, building up lumps or non-uniform wall thickness, variations in design of the final bulb will result. The beginner can experiment with such methods.

FOUR EXAMPLES: "GRAIN-OF-RICE" VASES

These vases are blown from heavy-walled tubing, with an outside diameter of one inch. The steps are as follows:

1. A point is pulled. When cool, it is scribed with the file, and then broken. The end is flame-polished lightly so as to make a smooth mouthpiece, or so that the rubber tubing of the swivel joint will slide on easily.

2. A section, about two inches long and adjacent to where the glass tapers to the point, is heated and thickened stepwise with slight pushing together. Care is taken to make it uniform for a smooth

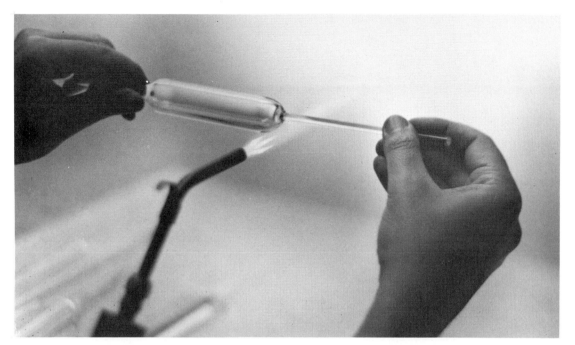

Figure 57. Attaching a handle to sealed-off tubing.

symmetric shape, or to introduce distortions if the shape is to be asymmetric.

3. A point is pulled at the other end of the thickened section. This is then heated and pulled off. The end is heated and blown out slightly, reheated, and shrunk back. This is repeated until a heavy wall is built up.

4. A 3/16-inch cane is attached to this end for a handle.

5. The procedure can be altered so that steps 3 and 4 follow 1, and then the tubing is thickened with step 2.

6. The center thickened section is reheated, with rotation, as uniformly as possible.

7. This is removed from the flame, and immediately inflated by blowing into the mouthpiece, rotating at the same time with the bulb almost horizontal.

8. The handle at the other end is used to pull to elongate the shape, or to push in to flatten it.

9. By heating the center in two separate steps, the vase with two bulbs can be formed.

10. To increase the asymmetry of some vases, additional glass can be applied to the wall to build up non-uniform thickness.

Examples are shown in figures 58 through 61.

Figure 58. "Vase Number 7."

Figure 59. "Biform Vase Number 5."

Figure 60. "Asymmetric Vase Number 3."

Figure 61. "Asymmetric Vase Number 4."

USE OF GLASS OBJECTS: "MINI-SCULPTURES," "FEELIES," HANDLES FOR DECORATIVE BOXES, JEWELRY, WIND CHIMES

A few examples of uses for glass objects made by flameworking techniques will be presented. Other uses will occur to the worker depending upon his own particular interests. There is a great pleasure in inventing or discovering applications or uses of one's work, so that this discussion will be very brief, rather than exhaustive in scope.

Some of the shapes illustrated are clearly small sculptures—perhaps "mini-sculptures" would be a good term—and their small size, displayed by mounting on a nicely proportioned block of wood, gives a pleasing and intimate feeling. The individual can absorb and master the object, rather than feel dwarfed by it.

Some objects, like the "Beach Stone," are pleasing to the touch as well as the eye. They make good "feelies," something to be picked up and held in the hand.

Other pieces fall into the area of jewelry. Many can be mounted in silver or gold, and represent imaginative fittings which could not be duplicated by lapidary techniques. Others can serve as decorative knobs or handles, mounted on boxes for cigarettes, cigarette lighters, and perfume bottles.

The blown shapes or shapes made from rather thin sheet glass fall into another class of uses. Vases, of course, are obvious, but they could also be assembled into wind chimes or hung as mobiles.

Part Three

FLAMEWORKING TORCHES AND OTHER EQUIPMENT

7. Basic Supplies

Very simple equipment is required to make the objects illustrated in this book. Basically, it consists of the flameworker's torch, a fuel (natural gas or propane), an oxidizing gas (air, for soft glass, and oxygen, for borosilicate glass), a few shaping tools, and a workbench with a fireproof top (asbestos board). If the bench is to be portable, a fairly compact design with drawer space is desirable, but if the bench is permanently located, a more sprawling design with tools left on the top of the bench is adequate.

8. The Work Bench

The simplest approach is to take a sturdy table or an existing workbench and convert it to a flameworker's bench. The top is covered with sheet asbestos board, which should be at least $3/8$ inch thick. Somewhat thicker asbestos board is more desirable but also more expensive. The oxygen tank is mounted at the side of the bench. It is convenient and safe to screw two large hooks into the side of the bench and loop a chain over them and around the tank. The oxygen tank and the propane tank stand on the floor. The torch and tools are on the bench top and the glass is stored in boxes, as shipped from the supplier, or in special racks built for that purpose.

A more advanced step would be to have drawer space for tools. This permits a cleaner table top and less delay while looking for the correct tool. Of course the beginner will want to store away some of his first examples in order to measure his progress later.

If the bench is to be portable, a more compact design is required, if only to move through doorways. The main requirement is adequate bench-top space. The design should have wheels with a mounted oxygen and gas tank, a manifold for the oxygen and gas, a vertical storage box for long glass, and drawers for tools and shorter pieces of glass.

9. *Fuels and Air or Oxygen*

For working borosilicate glass, propane or natural gas are suitable as fuels, and oxygen as the oxidizing agent. The propane can be stored in a camping or camp-trailer metal "bottle," holding about 25 pounds of liquid propane. It needs a simple reducing valve. The oxygen is purchased from a welding supply store. The cylinders are of different sizes. For some there is a demurrage charge; others can be leased. Typical weights and heights are given in the table below, for Linde cylinders, with the volume of oxygen gas at atmospheric pressure.

Table 1 : Oxygen Gas Cylinder Data

Code Number	Weight Empty	Weight Full	Height	Gas Volume
Q	65 lbs.	70 lbs.	35 in.	80 cu. ft.
D	116 lbs.	126 lbs.	48 in.	122 cu. ft.
S	80 lbs.	92 lbs.	51 in.	150 cu. ft.
K	133 lbs.	153 lbs.	56 in.	244 cu. ft.

The Q cylinder is somewhat small but of a convenient weight; the D cylinder is excessively heavy for the amount of oxygen it contains; the S weighs less and has more oxygen; the K cylinder is rather heavy and requires a special two-wheeled cart, with a curved back and protective chain, for easy handling.

The oxygen cylinder requires a reducing valve—a single-stage or two-stage valve—as the tank pressure as sold is about 2,200 pounds per square inch. The protective cap on the cylinder is unscrewed after properly mounting the tank at the workbench, using the protective chain. Then the main cylinder valve is opened very cautiously and gently, and closed quickly, letting out a small blast of gas just to clear any dirt out of the fittings (the fittings are almost always clean). Then the oxygen reducing valve is attached. Observe the direction of the threads in order to turn it correctly. Tighten it with a large crescent wrench (not a pipe wrench). The wrench should be adjusted correctly so as not to damage the hexagonal nut. This nut is then tightened firmly but not with great force.

The main cylinder valve is opened and the first pressure gauge should read 2,200 pounds per square inch. The intermediate valve is screwed in (it should have been turned out previously) until the second gauge reads 5-10 pounds per square inch. The beginner will have to experiment with controlling this valve and the valves at the torch. The outlet gas valve is then opened (both valves on the torch are closed off).

The valve of the propane tank is now opened. At this stage gas is available to the torch, as is oxygen. The steps of lighting and adjusting the torch flame will be discussed in Chapter 11. Here it will be noted that the gas valve of the torch is opened first, the flame is ignited, and then some oxygen is permitted to flow by opening the oxygen valve slightly.

For working soft glass, an air compressor is the source of supply for the air. It should have a storage tank to give a uniform, non-pulsing flow.

10. Cross Fires and Blast Lamps

There are several suppliers of flameworking torches. Each supplier has several designs, ranging from cross fires to small hand torches with only one size tip (see figure 62), to larger hand torches with several interchangeable tips (see figure 63), to the permanently mounted bench top model (see figure 64). This model is made of two concentric burners with separate controls. There is another type of burner, the ribbon burner, which is designed specially for heating a length of tubing uniformly in preparation for bending (see figure 65). As almost every object described in the text requires a finishing operation to remove the last handle or supporting rod, one of the hand-held torches is quite necessary.

The beginner can most easily start with the small hand torch and can then progress to the larger ones. By having a gas and oxygen manifold, he can then have two torches, the bench model and the hand torch, at one side. The latter is burning with a very small flame, ready for adjustment to any desired flame size for finishing operations.

The best torches now have certain safety features. That is, the gas and oxygen are brought right to the front of the torch in separate small tubes and the mixing is done right at the torch tip. In older types, the mixing was done farther back in the body of the torch. In that type, the flame could "flash back" and burn within the torch. One had to turn off the oxygen and gas immediately (and sometimes wait for the torch body to cool off, or it would "flash back" upon

Figure 62. Hand torch.

Figure 63. Hand torch with interchangeable tips.

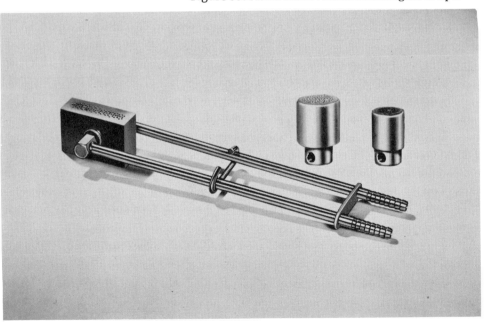

igniting) and then ignite again. With the new design, flashing back is impossible. There are small reamers for cleaning the tubes occasionally.

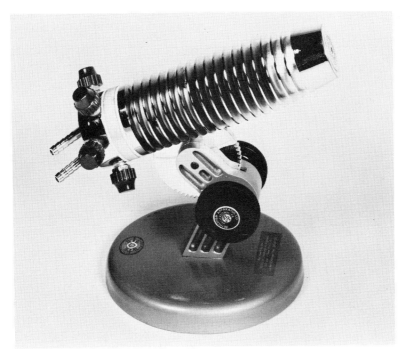

Figure 64. Bench-top model torch.

Figure 65. Ribbon burner.

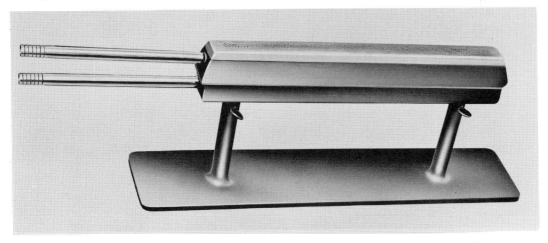

11. Lighting and Adjusting the Torch Flame

Anyone who has lighted a gas stove can operate the flameworking torch with ease. After adjusting the oxygen reducing valve as described, the exit valve is opened to let oxygen to the torch (both valves at the torch are shut off). Then the propane tank valve is opened. Incidentally, the tubing connecting gas and oxygen tanks with the torch should be good quality rubber or plastic tubing. There is a special plastic tubing with one tube orange and the other blue, sealed together. One strips them apart at each end to go to the separate connections, but leaves the major section sealed together to avoid tangling of the lines.

The propane valve at the torch is opened and the flame ignited. The gas flow is small at first so as not to "blow away" the flame. The flame is luminous yellow. The flame length is increased by opening the valve more, until the length is about 6 inches long, making sure that it is still burning close to the tip. The beginner should try various gas flows, and observe that the flame can be made to leave the tip of the torch.

The oxygen valve at the torch is then "cracked open" slightly, and the oxygen flow slowly increased. The beginner should observe the flame length and flame diameter with relative amounts of gas and air. To shut off the flame the oxygen valve is closed first, then the gas.

When adjusted for glassworking, there is a region of unburned gases close to the tip of the torch, shaped in the form of a cone or group of cones. The hottest region is about $1/2$ inch beyond the cones. With the small hand torch the flame can be made twelve inches long or more, or reduced to a very small flame of about one inch long, all with combined adjustment of gas and oxygen. The beginner should practice with controlling the gas and oxygen to adjust the flame size.

12. Accessories

The accessory tools can be very few and simple. They are some carbon rods, with tapered tips, some carbon plates (one with a handle to serve as a paddle), some insulating bricks on which to rest the carbon plates, forceps (preferably with protective wooden strips on the handles), tongs, glass-blowing swivel and mouthpiece, rubber tubing, corks, and Didymium glasses. The use of these tools has been described in the various operations.

Additional tools can be designed to meet specific needs—like special stamps to press into the surface of fluid glass. They can be carved in the end of a carbon rod, or out of wood (and the wood can be wetted). Special rollers to support long pieces of tubing can also be made.

13. Colors and Coloring of Glasses

There are two ways of obtaining colors in glass: one is to purchase colored glass, of the proper type (annealing point and coefficient of expansion should match), and the other is to fuse in colorants. The first method is by far the most satisfactory, for the colors are dissolved in the glass in a uniform manner. At present there is a wide range of colors available in soft glass (see Chapter 14) but only a limited range of colors available in the borosilicate glass. It is expected that more colors in the hard glass will become available to the hobbyist or craftsman as the demand increases.

There are two general classes of colors: transparent colors and opal colors. The latter should be capable of being reheated without losing their opal nature. Since the opal is a result of minute crystals scattering light, and since the numbers and sizes of the crystals depend upon heat treatment, reheating of some opals with a temperature cycle different from the production cycle can dissolve the crystals completely.

Coloring oxides can be purchased from a ceramic supply house. These are generally called "glaze stains" and are mixtures of oxides which have been fired and then ball-milled. These can be put inside a tube, and fused into the glass in a very hot flame. They do not really dissolve in the glass at these temperatures, but add color in a rather spotty manner, although this can produce some interesting patterns when added to clear glass or incorporated within. These glaze stains do have a wide range of colors. Of course, the small undissolved particles are regions of stress, and chances of cracking are increased.

A suggested minimum list of colors, which would extend the range of design, is as follows:

Table 2: Proposed Color List for Borosilicate Glasses

Transparent Colors	Opal Colors
Crystal	White
Black	
Brown	Corresponding colored
Purple	opals would be desirable,
Blue	to be incorporated inside
Green	crystal, or as a glass-
Yellow	maker's "mark."
Orange	
Red	

Most major suppliers of glass have the types of glass necessary for the beginner's use (see Appendix 3), and will gladly send catalogs upon request. Special glass colors, however, are indicated in the following table.

Table 3. Soft Colored Glass Rod*

Transparent	Opaque	Translucent
Crystal	Robin's Egg Blue	Alabaster
Amber	Opal	Alabaster Blue
Amethyst	Chalk White	Alabaster Green
Aquamarine	Navy	Alabaster Rose
Blue	Jade	
Green	Baby Blue	H-K Opaques
Rose Pink	Turquoise	(To weld with
Sel Ruby	Yellow	machine-made tube)
Gold Ruby	Orchid	
Black Crystal	Orange	White
Lead Crystal	Rose Pink	Apple Green
Yellow	Coral	Orange
	Red	Yellow
	Tan	Baby Blue
	Gray	Rose Pink
	Brown	
	Black	

86

* Available for Winding, Pressing and Blowing from Conlon Glass Associates, Inc., 10 Bethpage Road, Hicksville, N. Y., in ³⁄₈ to ¹⁄₂″ and ¹⁄₂ to ⁵⁄₈″ diameters.

Part Four

DESIGN

14. Introduction

Glass, as an artistic medium, fits nicely into contemporary trends of abstract and non-objective forms, of playing with light and color. The directness of working, the wonderfully smooth surfaces which develop before one's eyes in a living, organic manner all lend to an excitement of working and creating. In spite of the long history of flameworking, and the even longer history of free-blowing, the field of glassmaking is really unexplored. Specific examples had illustrated designs which were related to plants, or animals, or beach stones. In this discussion general principles will be stressed rather than specific examples.

Figure 66. "Glacier Ice."

15. Fractured Surfaces

Rough, fractured surfaces can be formed from massive pieces by rapid heating (heat shock). The surface formed will be shaped in an accidental manner, and may have very sharp edges. Such edges should be lightly fire-polished to smooth over. For example, a cane 1$^1/_4$ inches in diameter was fractured by too rapid heating, leaving a rough cone-like surface. A point was pulled several inches away to form a base, and with light fire-polishing of the sharp edges the sculpture was completed, followed by annealing (see figure 66).

16. Smooth Surfaces

By making use of the surface tension properties of fluid glass, amazingly smooth surfaces can be formed. The final shape formed depends on the initial starting shape and whether the fire-polishing was done very lightly or the glass was made quite fluid. Of course, by shaping with the carbon slabs, or by twisting and pulling, new shapes completely unrelated to the original can be formed.

17. Optical Effects

Using the above techniques, massive shapes produced from cane or from slabs can have smooth, lens-like surfaces—ranging from the simple lens of the "Anteater" (see figure 46), to a distorted spherical shape of the "Bimorph" (see figure 6), to the most complex combination of lenses of the "Whirling Dervish" (see figure 14), and the "Pine Cone" (see figure 1). Light shining on these surfaces is refracted, or bent, when it enters the surface. The light rays emerge and those which strike the eye produce the brilliant spot or sparkle. There is also wide variation in optical effects as one moves about and looks at the sculpture from different positions.

From the moment of heating the first piece of glass, the urge to play with designs is almost irresistible. The beginner can experiment with various designs and curvatures. While most of the shapes form convex to spherical lenses in a natural manner, some of the "stones" are bent to form concave lenses. One can experiment with different colored spotlights, different ways of mounting the sculpture, and different backgrounds. An example is a small colored light in the base support which will shine into the flattened bottom and be refracted at the surfaces. Or one might use the object or a set of objects to cast colored light patterns on a wall, with rotation producing dynamic and moving designs. Photography of glass is a special field in itself, and a person interested in photography might use the glass as a special tool to explore distorted and unusual color patterns.

18. Bubbles

Another effect, partly optical in nature and partly contributing to the design in special patterns, is the incorporation of bubbles into the sculpture. This element has been mentioned only slightly and has been left as a whole design area for the beginner to explore on his own. He can experiment with single bubbles, multiple bubbles, distorted bubbles, the procedures to make them spherical, and even more complex floating rings and floating designs. A design with a single bubble is shown in figure 67.

Figure 67. "The Wave."

19. *Limitations in Size and Shape*

Large pieces are difficult or awkward to hand-hold and construct, and may have to be clamped in a support. The more basic limitation can be described as "massiveness"— that is, the "thickness" of a sculpture. Even this thickness is difficult to define for very irregular shapes. The limitation goes back to annealing requirements—a large lump is difficult to anneal properly to reduce stress (unless one has an annealing furnace with programmed controller). From this one sees that small and intimate shapes can be "massive," and that larger pieces will be either spindly, with variations in thickness (see figure 68), sheet-like (although perhaps twisting and wandering rather than just flat), or blown hollow. Another possibility is to assemble several pieces together to build a larger sculpture (see figure 69).

The blown shapes, if made from tubing of uniform wall thickness, will tend to be thin-walled and have relatively little sparkle. More interesting directions are to emphasize this thinness, making very delicate shapes, or to distort the surface, adding or applying glass of varying thickness, embossing or stamping designs on the surface of applied glass, and then inflating. In the latter examples the tubing serves mainly as a support for other decorative elements.

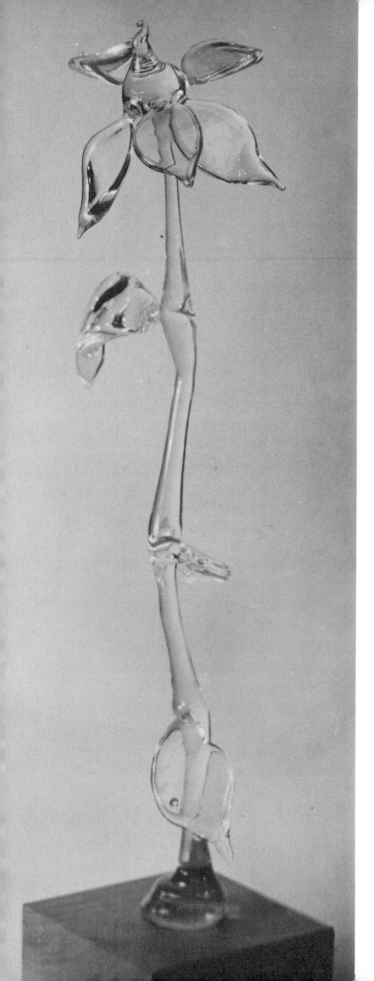

Figure 68. "Flower Number 3."

Figure 69. "Quartet."

20. Uniqueness

We return to the theme which introduced this book—the uniqueness of glass with its almost magical fluid properties and fire-polished surfaces. The marvelous "jewels" which can be formed most easily and the methods themselves capture the imagination. In most cases such objects could not even be created by a skilled worker with lapidary techniques, and those which could be duplicated by such techniques would take twenty to one hundred times as long to execute.

The beginner can easily shape small sculptures —"mini-sculptures"— or make shapes pleasing to the touch, or abstractions of plants and animals. The creatures of the sea and insects have been unexplored in this book. The beginner can create a world of fantasy which sparkles in the light. These objects can be used as pure, decorative sculpture or in many other ways, only a few of which were suggested.

The worker is excited by the manipulation of the glass and by the awareness that the flame and glass are very hot, with a feeling of danger—although one very quickly gets used to the idea of being close to the flame. To the worker, the "doing" is the thing—whether he attempts to make a piece according to some preconceived idea or sketch, or whether he creates in the flame itself, making use of each twist and bend and fortunate accident.

Sea Creature

Anteater

Dancing Dervish

Whirling Dervish

Quartet

Sea Creature

Sea Anemone

Glacier Ice

Part Five

THE STORY OF FLAMEWORKER'S GLASS

21. The Small Glass Factory

While the flameworker need never know how his glass is prepared, or what the constituents are that make up his glasses, it does seem very desirable to make such information easily available to him. This discussion will also give him greater understanding if he should have the opportunity to visit a glass factory in America or Europe. The small glass factory with the free-blowing team or "shop" is much more exciting than the modern production factory with automatic machinery. With the team all the operations can be clearly seen and described. The wonderful skill and coordination of the workers can be observed.

22. Methods and Techniques

OXIDE COMPOSITION OF THE GLASS

One begins in the factory with the composition of the glass (or glasses) to be melted. The basic composition can be expressed in terms of weight percents of the oxides which will eventually be derived from the batch materials during the melting process. For purposes of illustration, a base glass can be chosen from the family of "lead" glasses, or to be more precise, from glasses containing lead oxide (" 'Tis a concrete of salt and sand or stones"). Such artistic glasses contain about 30-36 percent lead oxide (PbO), 10-13 percent potassium oxide (K_2O), and 53-56 percent sand or silica (SiO_2). More specifically, a base glass can be:

Lead oxide	PbO	30.0%
Potassium oxide	K_2O	15.0
Silica	SiO_2	55.0
		100.0%

To this clear or "crystal" base composition, one adds certain oxides to produce colors, like cobalt oxide, iron oxide, uranium oxide, etc.; other ingredients to produce translucent glass ("opals"); and others to aid in the removal of bubbles during the melting process, such removal of bubbles being called "fining." If these ingredients are added, additional adjustments in the relative proportions of the above three oxides may be necessary so as to maintain certain desired physical properties, which would have been altered slightly by the oxide colorants or opalizing agents.

102

For purposes of comparison, another composition, that of a boro-silicate glass, is:

Sodium oxide	Na_2O	3.8%
Potassium oxide	K_2O	0.4
Boric oxide	B_2O_3	12.9
Aluminum oxide	Al_2O_3	2.2
Silica	SiO_2	80.7
		100.0%

This glass is the one most commonly used in scientific flameworking, and has several advantages, which were described earlier, for artistic flameworking as well as for the fabrication of scientific apparatus.

BATCH COMPOSITION

The next step is to convert the above percentage, using weight of oxides, to weight of raw materials used, with an arbitrary "size of batch." That is, the oxides may be supplied by some more complex material. For example, potassium carbonate (K_2CO_3) may yield the potassium oxide (K_2O) after the melting process has taken place and carbon dioxide (CO_2) has been evolved. One knows by experience the materials that will be used to supply these oxides (there are lists of such materials in books on industrial glass manufacture). The weight percent of oxide yielded from the selected batch material is known by chemical analysis (for example, pearl ash yields 57.0 percent potassium oxide), and thus the amount of raw materials can be calculated to give the desired weight of glass. Thus:

Lead oxide	Pb_3O_4	26.9
Pearl ash	$K_2CO_3 \cdot 3/2H_2O$	15.4
Potassium nitrate	KNO_3	9.4
Silica	SiO_2	48.2
		99.9
		(relative weight)

is exactly equivalent to the lead base glass presented above.

103

RAW MATERIALS

Many raw materials can be used in glassmaking, but their ultimate function is to furnish the oxides which will remain after they decompose, oxides like SiO_2, K_2O, PbO, boric oxide (B_2O_3), aluminum oxide (Al_2O_3), and sodium oxide (Na_2O). A book on glass manufacture will give a list of various raw materials, with the common name, scientific name, chemical formula, oxide yielded after decomposition, and the weight percent of oxide yielded. The oxides have different functions, with SiO_2 playing the key role, that of the "glass-former."

Figure 70. Glassblowing tools.

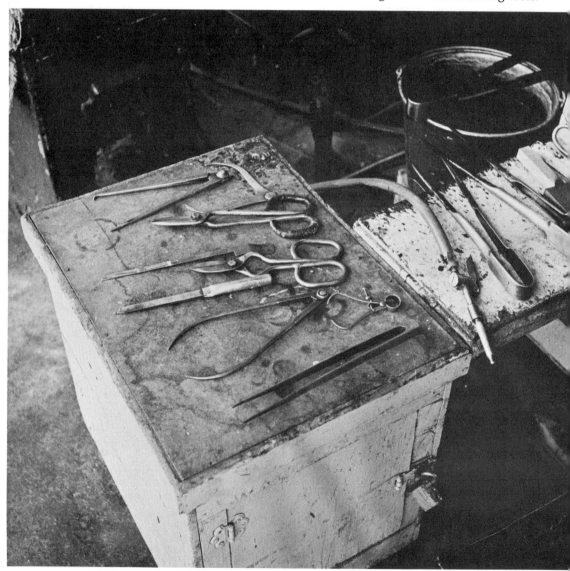

FURNACES, GLASS MELTING POTS, AND GLASSMAKING TOOLS

There are three types of glass melting furnaces, each attempting to meet a different need. It will become apparent that they are not strictly comparable. "Pot" furnaces vary in size, and hold from one to sixteen ceramic containers, called "pots." If more than one is used, then different colored glasses can be melted at the same time, which is a requirement for most artistic glass production. The second type, the "day tank," is a batch melting furnace. The third type, used in large factory production, is the "continuous tank." As its name suggests, it has raw materials entering one end periodically and melted glass removed continuously at the other end to make bottles, sheet glass, tubing, television tube face plates, and so on. In the day tank and the continuous tank the refractory walls also serve as the walls of the container to hold the molten glass. Only one color at a time can be melted in those units. They usually hold more glass than does a single pot.

A crucible, which is really a small pot, can hold as little as a fraction of a pound, while a large pot can hold as much as 3,000 pounds of glass. Day tanks can hold from pounds to several tons of glass. Continuous tanks can hold several hundred pounds to several hundred tons and can yield glass from pounds per hour to tons per hour.

There are a number of tools used in the small factory for the operation of a pot furnace or day tank. There is a large fork mounted on wheels for moving the heavy pots outside of the furnace. There are ladles and rakes for cleaning the surface of the glass, or for removing the glass at the bottom of an almost empty pot. Such glass cannot be utilized and must be removed prior to refilling with batch.

105

FREE-BLOWING

In the factory system there is a group of men, called the "shop," who operate as a team (see figure 70). Only a few tools are used now, as in ancient times, when blowing was first invented. (A most interesting description of glassmaking of the period about 1100 A.D. is in Theophilus Rugerus, *The Various Arts*, translated by C. R. Dodwell, London, 1961). These tools will be described below.

BLOWIRON AND PUNTY

The blowiron is used to "gather" the glass out of the pot or tank. The blowiron is a long hollow iron tube, about four feet in length. The workman holds it at the end and dips the other end, which has a slightly enlarged "nose," into the glass. He rotates the iron, winding up a gob or "gather" of glass. Later he can inflate the glass by blowing into the mouthpiece when he comes to that stage of the operation. Other procedures could be carried out with an additional blowiron, but customarily another tool is used instead, the punty (French *pontil*). This is a solid iron rod, also about four feet long, which costs somewhat less than the hollow iron. It was probably developed simply because it was cheaper. With the punty the workman can gather glass and apply it or "lay" it onto a blown shape. The punty can be attached or sealed to the bottom of a blown vessel on the blowiron and the vessel can then be severed or "cracked off" the blowiron.

MARVER, FORMING BLOCK, BOARD, WOODJACK, SHEARS

These are the tools for controlling the shape of the gather before blowing, and for controlling and altering the shape during the blowing process. The gather at the end of the blowiron is rolled or "marvered" on the marver table, which is a polished iron slab. This marvering permits shaping the gather into a cylindrical form and chilling the surface somewhat (see figure 71). If a spherical form is desired, then the gather is rotated in a wetted wooden block with a hollowed hemispherical form. If the glass is sufficiently hot so that it flows easily, cooling the surface with water cannot set up any stresses. Thus at this temperature the glass will not crack, and the water is turned to steam. This also chills the surface, an operation which apparently gives control during the inflation step.

Figure 71. Marvering: Step 1.

After the preliminary shaping, the gather can be inflated. The shape is controlled by rubbing with a wooden board (the worker sits in the "chair") and by the pincers or woodjacks, along with rotation of the vessel by rolling the blowiron on the arms of the chair. In addition, the action of gravity is to stretch the hot glass, if it hangs down, or flatten it, if it is held upright. The woodjacks are pincers with wooden tips.

After the vessel is blown to size, the punty can be attached directly opposite the blowiron nose, at what will become the base, and the glass severed from the blowiron by chilling it there and

107

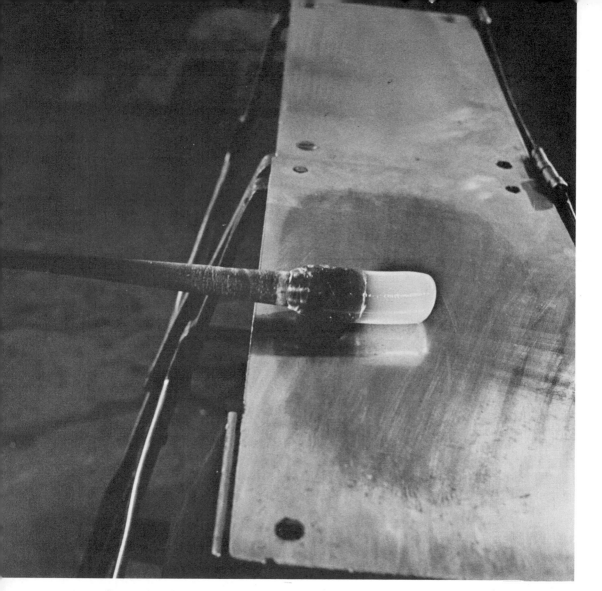

Figure 72. Marvering: Step 2.

striking the iron a blow with a metal rod. It can be reheated and
the opening, where the blowiron had been attached, can be enlarged
and cut down with a shears (amazingly enough!). The shape can be
spun out into a disk, if desired, by centrifugal force. It can be
shaped, using the board, woodjack, and pincers.

REHEATING FURNACE

The process of shaping the glass takes some time so that it cools
while being worked, becoming less fluid until it can no longer be
deformed. Therefore it is reheated periodically by inserting the glass,
and of course the tip of the iron, into the furnace opening at the pot

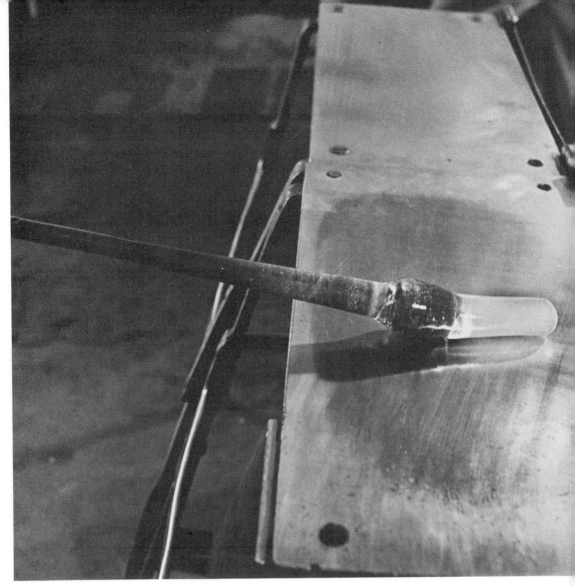

Figure 73. Marvering: Step 3.

or into a special reheating furnace called the "glory hole." Use of the reheating furnace is common practice now. The handle of the iron may become too hot to hold and water may have to be sprayed onto it. Further, the point where the glass is sealed to the iron should not become too hot, as then the whole vessel can fall or flow right off the iron.

109

THE FREE-BLOWING TEAM: THE "SHOP"

Customarily there are five men who work together in a group or team called a "shop." The "gaffer" is the master glass blower, who sits in the wooden "chair," which has two elongated arms. He

Figure 74. Gaffer at work.

rotates the blowiron or punty on these arms during the shaping of the article (see figure 74.) As he rotates the iron he applies the various tools described, the board, woodjack, or forming block, or uses the shears (but then rotates more slowly as he is cutting glass at the same time). The "servitor" is his chief assistant. He makes the initial gather and does the preliminary shaping at the marver table. The "blower" is the second assistant who carries it one step further before handing it to the gaffer. Thus considerable work may be done on the object before the gaffer actually takes over. The "bit-gatherer" gathers small gobs of glass for application of handles, legs, feet, knobs, and so on. He comes and holds the iron with the glass close to the object. The gaffer seizes it with tongs, and guides it into position above the object, which he also controls and rotates as necessary, combining both actions during the application of glass.

The "taker-in" carries the finished article to a furnace, called a "lehr," for controlled cooling.

ANNEALING

The controlled cooling process mentioned above is called annealing. After the object is completed, it must be held for a while at the "annealing temperature" or "annealing point," even reheating to that temperature if necessary, or cooling if the object is at a higher temperature just after working. After the holding period, it is then cooled gradually, and if done properly, the stresses in the glass are reduced to a minimum. Thus it is less likely to break. The subject of annealing is discussed in greater detail in Appendix 2.

PREPARATION OF GLASS FOR THE FLAMEWORKER: CANE AND TUBING

The preparation of cane or tubing is one of the most interesting operations to watch in the small factory. For making cane or tubing a very large amount of glass, weighing 50 to 80 pounds, is gathered and marvered into a conical shape, four to eight inches in diameter at the larger end and about twelve inches long. The flat end is dropped firmly against a hot iron disk carried by a helper, so that each end is firmly supported. For the cane, the man holding the gather walks backwards stretching the glass into a rod. The glass sags down and touches slats on the floor. Usually a third workman measure the diameter with calipers and fans that portion of the glass of the correct diameter so as to cool it and make it rigid. The glass continues to stretch out of the hot gather on the iron. A rod one hundred feet long can be made, of approximately uniform diameter, although the end sections are non-uniform.

For the tubing, a bubble of small diameter is blown almost through the entire length of the gather. Again the glass is attached to the hot iron disk, and the blower walks backwards away from the helper. He blows intermittently to keep the tubing round, and again a third workman measures the diameter and fans the glass. The whole process is quite amazing and depends on good coordination and judgment.

111

Appendices

1. Some Physical Properties of Glass

There are several physical properties of glass which are important for the flameworker. Everyone is aware that glass is a brittle material (" 'Tis friable when cold, which made our proverb, As brittle as glass.") and almost everyone is aware that it deforms and flows at high temperatures ("When melted 'tis tenacious and sticks together. 'Tis ductile whilst red hot, and fashionable into any form, but not malleable, and may be blown into a hollowness."). Most people are not aware that there is a surface tension property and an expansion-temperature property, both important to the working of glass. These different properties will be discussed below.

1. BRITTLENESS WHEN COLD

A piece of glass, no matter what its shape—whether sheet or rod or tubing or bottle—is a single material or a monolithic piece, in contrast to many stones which are aggregates or polycrystalline. A fracture, once started, can move or propagate through the piece, if it is under stress. It can travel an apparently erratic and wandering path, giving a smooth surface to the fracture, with some irregularities or small waves.

Because of its brittleness, and its monolithic nature, glass is broken, sawn, ground, scratched, and engraved by various techniques. In all cases the intention is to control the process and not have the glass fracture in some uncontrolled manner in the wrong place.

2. FLOW-DEFORMATION PROPERTIES WHEN HOT

The ductility of glass when hot is of prime importance. Glass, in cooling, becomes less fluid, although the degree of fluidity of a glass at a given temperature will depend upon the composition, which can vary widely (composition variations are shown in the examples of the lead glass and the borosilicate glass, section 7). This degree of fluidity can be measured experimentally, and thus it is possible to compare different glasses.

3. FLUIDITY-TEMPERATURE

This fluidity, or ease of flow, and its dependence on temperature can be made more familiar. Some glasses can be as fluid, at 1400-1600°C (2550-2910°F), as No. 20 motor oil is at room temperature. Of course different compositions vary—some, when heated to 1400-1600°C, might be as fluid as water. Upon cooling, the fluidity decreases and at about 800°C (1470°F) the glass can be in a taffy-like state, becoming almost rigid at a lower temperature, about 450°C (840°F). Glass deforms slowly if held at that temperature, with slight changes in shape over a period of hours. Finally, at a lower temperature glass becomes a rigid and brittle material—the shape made at a higher temperature is now "frozen-in."

4. FLUIDITY-VISCOSITY

In scientific studies on glass, the term "viscosity" is used rather than fluidity. Both terms are qualitative and descriptive and they have an inverse relationship. That is to say, at high temperatures glass is very fluid—it has a *high* fluidity, but a *low* viscosity; as it cools the glass becomes less fluid—it has a low fluidity and a high viscosity.

116

5. VISCOSITY COEFFICIENT AND TEMPERATURE

One must somehow make quantitative, experimental measurements on the viscosity of glasses if different ones are to be compared and arranged in some ordered manner. There is a "measure" quantity—the coefficient of viscosity—which can be defined and measured over a wide range of temperatures.

6. EXPERIMENTAL RESULTS: THE "POINTS" WHICH ARE IMPORTANT

The results of the experiments can be plotted in the form of a graph. In practice, however, one considers a few defined "points" on this graph. That is, at three different numerical values of the viscosity coefficient, which are given the names "strain" viscosity, "annealing" viscosity, and "softening" viscosity, the temperatures which correspond to these points are tabulated. Thus the temperatures are given names analogous to freezing point and boiling point, namely, "strain point," "annealing point," and "softening point."

The above points are really most pertinent to the controlled cooling process, or annealing. A fourth point is related to the working process of glass. This is called the "working point," and naturally is at a higher temperature than the others and thus at a higher fluidity and a lower viscosity. Actually, the glass can be worked over a range of temperatures about the "working point"— this is called the "working range." (See figure 75 for data on several glasses).

7. THE "WORKABILITY" OF GLASS: COMPARISON BETWEEN LEAD GLASS AND BOROSILICATE GLASS

With the first piece of glass heated in the torch flame, the beginner will get a feel for the "working range." The glass will become fluid, and both hands will have to be coordinated to rotate and control the heated region. Upon withdrawing the glass from the flame, it can still be pulled or twisted for some seconds, as it cools through the "working range." An interesting comparison can be made between a lead glass and the borosilicate glass. Starting with rods of the same diameter (5/8-inch diameter) the borosilicate rod must be heated to cherry red to orange in color and then can be pulled out slowly for about 12 seconds, while the lead glass, with a working range at a lower temperature where it is only dull red in color, can

117

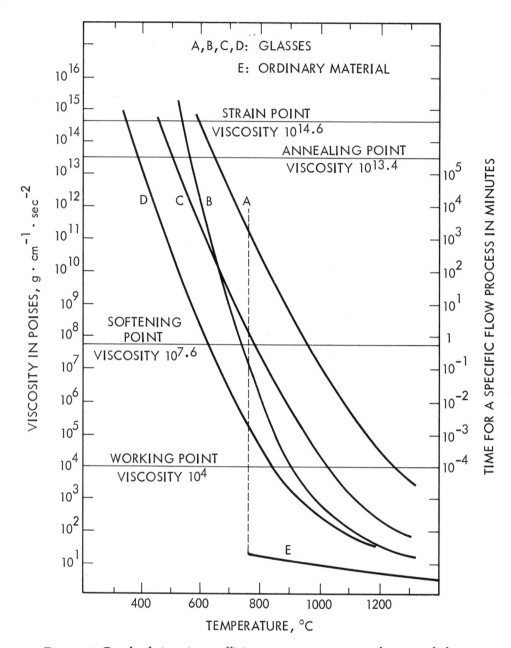

Figure 75. Graph of viscosity coefficient versus temperature for several glasses.

be pulled out slowly for about 20 seconds. The higher temperature rod cools quickly, losing heat by radiation; the lower temperature rod also cools by radiation but more slowly. Thus the lead glass has better working properties in the sense that there is more time to do an operation.

8. SURFACE TENSION PROPERTY

The surface tension property is another key property. As softened glass behaves like a liquid, its surface tension tends to deform it in such a manner that its total surface is decreased—the net effect is to round off surfaces and give a smoothness to them. A bubble in the interior will tend to become a sphere if the glass is fluid enough (see figure 67). Thus the surfaces are "fire-polished" in a most unique manner.

9. EXPANSION-TEMPERATURE RELATION

The expansion-temperature relation, commonly called "thermal expansion," is a property of glass and of other rigid materials. The piece simply changes length with temperature, expanding as the temperature is raised, and contracting as the temperature is lowered. This expansion may vary considerably with composition. Fused silica has a very low expansion, borosilicate glasses higher, lead oxide and soda-lime glasses higher yet. Actually these expansions are very small: a typical soda-lime glass rod, 10 cm long, will expand only 0.035 cm on being heated from 0° to 400°C (32° to 750°F).

10. USE OF "SOFT" AND "HARD" (BOROSILICATE) GLASSES

The lower working temperature lead glass (or lime glass) is called a "soft" glass, while the higher working temperature borosilicate glass is called a "hard" glass. There are advantages and disadvantages to each glass.

If one could invent a "best" glass it would have a low softening point and therefore cool slowly (by radiation) and give the worker a long time to manipulate and shape a piece. Further, it would have a low coefficient of expansion; zero would be best for then it could be heated without any change of dimension and no stress between hot regions and cool regions. These two properties, low softening point and low expansion, are incompatible with conventional compositions. Therefore some kind of compromise is necessary.

The "soft" glass has good working properties but it has high expansion, and must be heated carefully, or it will crack, and must also be cooled carefully, or it will crack upon cooling. In flameworking techniques, in which a piece is heated non-uniformly (after all, cool parts are held in the hands and the center is red hot), it is difficult to make massive pieces of a soft glass, as the stresses will be severe. (In free-blowing, with a lead glass, the piece is heated throughout in a uniform manner at the end of the blowiron or on the punty iron.)

The "hard" glass has poorer working properties, and requires higher temperatures (gas with oxygen, rather than gas with air), but the low expansion property means more rapid heating with a minimum of preheating. In addition, greater extremes of temperature from the hot region to the cool region are acceptable, and annealing or controlled cooling is simpler. Scientific laboratory glass has become exclusively borosilicate, for its advantages far outweigh its working disadvantages (see Chapter 3, A Brief History of Flameworking).

2. *Annealing Procedures and Annealing Furnaces*

1. PRINCIPLES OF ANNEALING

If glass is cooled quickly to room temperature following working at elevated temperatures, in flameworking techniques or offhand techniques, the piece will have high stresses and crack apart, or if no cracks form immediately, it will be very sensitive to a slight additional stress and a crack may form after a while ("Breaks being thin without annealing"). The sensitivity to fracture can be reduced with a proper cooling treatment. This proper cooling treatment is called "annealing."

That annealing was a desirable procedure was known in ancient times. Theophilus, in about 1140 A.D. described The Annealing Kiln, and how objects are put into "the annealing kiln, which should be moderately heated." (See Theophilus Rugerus, *The Various Arts*, translated by C. R. Dodwell, London, 1961.) This book on diverse arts, including glassmaking, is to be recommended as a most interesting historical document on the crafts and craftsmanship.

During annealing the glass is kept or "soaked" at an elevated temperature (the "annealing" point, described in Appendix 1) for a while—about 20 minutes—and then cooled slowly. The furnace in which this is done commercially is called a "lehr," but here it will be called an annealing furnace. It is obvious that if the temperature of the object has dropped below the annealing point, then the object will have to be heated and "soaked," and if the temperature is above the annealing point, the object will have to be cooled and soaked.

2. TEMPERATURE-TIME CYCLES

The complete process consists of a heating step, which must not be so rapid as to break the object, a "soaking" step which will relieve stresses introduced from the heating, a cooling step in the high temperature region to about 75°C below the annealing point, and a cooling step from there to room temperature. Both of the cooling steps are to be slow enough that stress can be partially relieved and not become too great.

The overall temperature-time cycle is shown in figure 76. There is a formula for the heating rate and cooling rate. This formula at first

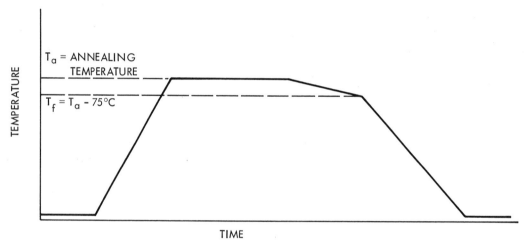

Figure 76. Overall temperature-time cycle for annealing.

appears very complicated, but by substitution of the proper physical constants it can be reduced to a much simpler form. In the simpler form it involves the stress level, S, the coefficient of expansion, α, and the thickness of the object, A. For heating a relative high value of stress, S can be used. For cooling, the same basic formula applies, but a lower value of S is used, and in the high temperature step, a different values of the coefficient of expansion, α, is used. In the final cooling step, another value of S is used and the coefficient of expansion of 0-300°C range is used. In all three cases, the thickness, A, is of course the same. Therefore, the formula (see footnote) can be reduced to:

For heating rate: R_h (degrees centigrade/minute) $=$

$$\frac{S}{69(\alpha \cdot 10^7)A^2}$$

and the cooling steps can be related directly to the heating rate formula by:

For high temperature cooling: $R^* = R_h/11.2$
For lower temperature cooling: $R_f = R_h/1.4$

From these formulas, one can build up simple tables for the heating rate and for the two cooling rates. The tables will depend upon the coefficient of expansion, and thus there will be a borosilicate glass value (32×10^{-7} cm/cm/°C) and a soft glass value (95×10^{-7} cm/cm/°C). The value of S for heating is 1400 psi, and the value for S for cooling in the high temperature region, namely 250 psi, has already been incorporated into the formula:

$$R^* = R_h/11.2$$

as has the value for S for cooling in the lower temperature region, namely 1000 psi, been incorporated into the formula

$$R_f = R_h/1.4$$

Now as the basic heating formula involves the thickness of the glass, A, in inches, the simple tables must also display this relationship.

All three tables have the same format, namely:

R_h or R^* or R_f (degrees centigrade/minute)
Type of glass (actually the α, coefficient of expansion)
Thickness, A (inches) $^1/_4$ $^1/_2$ 1   2   4
Corresponding R_h or R^* or R_f —   —   —   —   —

---

* The rate of cooling or heating is related to the corresponding stress introduced (in an elastic body) by:

$$R = \frac{24\,k\,(1-\sigma)}{\alpha \cdot A^2}\,\frac{S}{E} \cdot 60$$

where:
$R =$ rate of temperature change, degrees centigrade/minute
$k =$ thermal diffusivity (0.00077 in²/sec when A is in inches)
$\sigma =$ Poisson's ratio (0.22, so that $1 - \sigma$ is 0.78)
$\alpha =$ coefficient of expansion at the prevailing temperature
$A =$ thickness to be considered, in inches
$S =$ stress in the central plane, being compression on cooling and tension on heating
$E =$ Young's modulus (10^7 psi)

The tables are displayed below (see Tables 4 through 6).

For heating:

Table 4 for R_h

	"Hard" Glass with $\alpha = 32 \times 10^{-7}$ cm/cm/°C					"Soft" Glass with $\alpha = 95 \times 10^{-7}$ cm/cm/°C				
Thickness (inches)	$1/4$	$1/2$	1	2	4	$1/4$	$1/2$	1	2	4
Corresponding R_h (°C/min.)	600	150	40	9	2.5	200	50	13	3	0.8

For high temperature cooling:

Table 5 for R^* (Note: $R^* = R_h/11.2$)

	"Hard" Glass with $\alpha = 32 \times 10^{-7}$ cm/cm/°C					"Soft" Glass with $\alpha = 95 \times 10^{-7}$ cm/cm/°C				
Thickness (inches)	$1/4$	$1/2$	1	2	4	$1/4$	$1/2$	1	2	4
Corresponding R^* (°C/min.)	54	13.5	3.3	0.8	0.2	18	4.5	1.1	0.27	0.07

For final, low temperature cooling:

Table 6 for R_f (Note: $R_f = R_h/1.4 = 8R^*$)

	"Hard" Glass with $\alpha = 32 \times 10^{-7}$ cm/cm/°C					"Soft" Glass with $\alpha = 95 \times 10^{-7}$ cm/cm/°C				
Thickness (inches)	$1/4$	$1/2$	1	2	4	$1/4$	$1/2$	1	2	4
Corresponding R_f (°C/min.)	430	100	30	6.5	1.6	140	30	9	21	5.6

The use of the tables is very simple.
1. First note whether your glass is "hard" or "soft."
2. Look up the annealing temperature for the upper temperature.
3. Calculate T_f as annealing temperature less 75°C.
4. Estimate the thickness of the piece you will make.
5. Now look for the corresponding heating and cooling rates, R_h, R^*, and R_f.
6. Using the temperatures and rates, draw the temperature-time cycle curve. This involves simple calculations going from rates to time, after drawing in horizontal lines for the temperatures.

The application of these ideas will be made clearer in a specific example which follows.

A particular example of the use of the tables is as follows:

1. Hard glass
2. The annealing temperature is found to be $T_a = 560°C$
3. $T_a - 75°C = T_f = 485°C$
4. Consider that the piece is 1 inch thick
5. The cooling and heating rates are found in the tables:

$R_h = 40°C/minute$

$R^* = 3.3°C/minute$

$R_f = 30°C/minute$

6. The time of heating, t_h, from room temperature, which is about 20°C, to $T_a = 560°C$, at $R_h = 40°C/minute$, the time of cooling, t^*, from $T_a = 560°C$ to $T_a - 75°C = T_f = 485°C$, at $R^* = 3.3°C/minute$, and the time of cooling, t_f, from T_f to room temperature at $R_f = 30°C/minute$ are given by:

$$t_h = \frac{520°C}{40°C/minute} = 13 \text{ minutes}$$

$$t^* = \frac{75°C}{3.3°C/minute} = 23 \text{ minutes}$$

$$t_f = \frac{485°C}{30°C/minute} = 16 \text{ minutes}$$

The graph looks like this (see figure 77):

Figure 77. Annealing time for one-inch-thick borosilicate specimen.

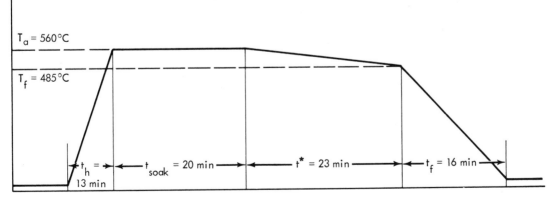

3. FLAME ANNEALING

A simple annealing procedure, called flame annealing, is to heat the finished object fairly uniformly with a bushy flame, then decrease the flame temperature by cutting off the oxygen almost completely and continue to heat the object. Soot is deposited on the object under these conditions. One continues to heat for several minutes, and then puts the object in a place free of drafts, on an insulating material. This procedure proves adequate for thin or small pieces.

4. SIMPLEST ANNEALING UNIT

The simplest annealing unit is a large tin can partially filled with Vermiculite. After finishing and reheating fairly uniformly by flame annealing, the object is placed in a shallow hole in the Vermiculite. More is then poured on top to cover it. The Vermiculite is a good heat insulator, so the object cools very slowly, approximating an annealing cycle. The object can be too hot to touch after thirty minutes, and should be left until cool. Several such cans permit making many objects in succession without any need to remove the first object made.

5. ANNEALING FURNACES AND CONTROLLERS

For more careful annealing, a requirement for large pieces (or if one wishes to sell his work, and not have complaints), a furnace with a controller is required. Commercial electric pottery kilns are available, and they can be equipped with a controller. There are many controllers available commercially. Some pottery kiln suppliers sell a complete glass-annealing furnace with controller.

126 Typically, the procedure with a furnace is to flame-anneal and place the cool objects into the cold furnace on a bed of Vermiculite. Then after the furnace is full, the annealing cycle is followed, as determined by the thickest piece.

3. List of Suppliers

TORCHES

Bethlehem Apparatus Company, Inc.
Hellertown, Pennsylvania

Eisler Engineering Co.
740-770 South 13th Street
Newark, New Jersey

ACCESSORIES

Bethlehem Apparatus Company, Inc.
Hellertown, Pennsylvania

Eisler Engineering Co.
740-770 South 13th Street
Newark, New Jersey

L. O. Bucher
Glassmaking Accessories
3874 Crescent Drive
Santa Barbara, California

GLASS

Soft Glass:
Conlon Glass Associates, Inc.
10 Bethpage Road
Hicksville, New York 11802

Borosilicate Glass and Soft
or "Flint" Glass:
Kimble Laboratory Glassware
Owens-Illinois Glass Company
(Order through nearest dealer)

Borosilicate Glass and Soft
or "Flint" Glass
Corning Glass Works
(Order through nearest dealer)

ANNEALING FURNACES

Cress Electric Furnaces
Recco Equipment Company
323 W. Maple Ave.
Monrovia, California 91016

Wilt
Laboratory Glass Blowing, Inc.
860 Albany-Shaker Road
Lathan, New York 12110

Index

Frederic Schuler

has long been interested in science and in art and, in addition to following a scientific career in industry and teaching—he teaches engineering, physics and chemistry at Santa Barbara City College, Santa Barbara, California—he has found time for work in such diverse forms as sculpture, ceramics and glassblowing.

He became interested in glassblowing over twenty years ago, while working at Oak Ridge, Tennessee. There he started to work on his own in the evenings and on Sundays. When he returned to the University of Wisconsin for graduate study in physical chemistry, he did some glassblowing as part of his research work.

In 1953 he joined the Corning Glass Works Research Laboratory. His interest in glassmaking was strengthened by the general exposure to glass factory operations and artistic glassmaking at Steuben Glass, which was located nearby. His specific interests were strengthened by his research studies on photosensitive glass, which had artistic, decorative and architectural potentials.

Dr. Schuler then joined the Corning Museum of Glass and was in charge of its program on ancient glass technical studies. This work led to the idea of comprehensive studies on techniques for the artist-craftsman. He saw the need for details recording techniques by combining text and photographs. Frederic Carder, the founder of Steuben Glass, then aged ninety-three, was very helpful to him. Dr. Schuler did work in his workshop and they discussed many techniques in great detail, including ones which have never been described in print.

Born in Monroe, Wisconsin, Dr. Schuler did his undergraduate and graduate work at the University of Wisconsin. He now lives in Santa Barbara, California, with his wife and four children. *Flameworking* is the first of a projected series of books on glassmaking for the craftsman.